Realistic Animation, Lighting & Sound

21 Projects for Your Model Railroad

Selected by Kent Johnson

KALMBACH
BOOKS

Printed in the United States of America

2000 01 02 03 04 05 06 07 08   10 9 8 7 6 5 4 3 2 1

Visit our website at
http://kalmbachbooks.com
Secure online ordering available

Publisher's Cataloging in Publication
(Provided by Quality Books, Inc.)

Realistic animation, lighting & sound : 21 projects for
your model railroad / selected by Kent Johnson. —
1st ed.
p. cm.
ISBN: 0-89024-338-7

1. Railroads—Models. I. Johnson, Kent J.,
1968-

TF197.R43 2000   625.1'9
                                       QBI99-1841

Book design: Jennifer Gaertner
Cover design: Kristi Ludwig

The material in this book has previously appeared as articles in *Model Railroader* Magazine. Most are reprinted in their entirety and may include an occasional reference to an item elsewhere in the same issue or in a previous issue.

CONTENTS

ANIMATION

LIGHTING

SOUND

1

Animation on the Lone Pine & Tonopah RR

By Kermit Paul and Ken Sullivan

REALISTIC SCALE ANIMATION INCREASES THE OPERATORS'
ENJOYMENT AND SPECTATOR APPEAL OF THE HO SCALE
LONE PINE & TONOPAH RR. THE CHALLENGE IS TO CREATE ANIMATION
THAT OPERATES SMOOTHLY, WITHOUT ANY QUICK OR JERKY
MOVEMENTS THAT DESTROY THE ILLUSION.

Motion devices

Animation is a combination of mechanical and lighting effects that give the appearance of purposeful motion. While some of our examples may seem complex, all of these devices break down into simple applications of basic principles. Construction of these mechanisms is relatively easy, and great precision isn't required.

Quiet, slow-speed geared motors are the heart of all these animation devices. Their slow rotary motion can be converted to linear (back and forth) or angular motion, using the methods shown in fig. 1. When rotary motion is necessary, it can be transmitted using cams, chains and sprockets, or belts and pulleys.

I use mechanical animation to operate a number of devices on the LP&T:

- Dancers moving inside the USO dance hall
  - Log dump at the mill pond
  - Log loader in the woods
  - Moving automobiles
  - Rocker-style oil pumps
  - Rotating oil and water spouts for locomotives
  - Sawmill carriage and saws
  - Sawmill log chain
  - Scrap-metal loading crane
  - Semaphore signals

Motion can also be created by using flashing or flickering lights to simulate fires, electric arc welders, emergency vehicle lights, traffic lights, and similar items. By sequencing the lights, it's possible to reproduce

Left: The Sullivan Lumber Co. at Coaldale was scratchbuilt by Ken Sullivan almost 30 years ago. It incorporates an operating drag chain to pull logs into the mill, spinning circular saw blades, a movable saw carriage, and a "green" chain where the finished lumber is delivered and graded.

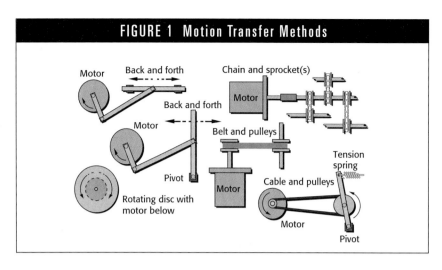

FIGURE 1 Motion Transfer Methods

industrial signs and theater chase lights. Examples of these lighting effects are incorporated into:

- Day-to-night changes in the layout room lighting
  - Hobo campfire
  - House on fire
  - Neon signs
  - Sawdust burner
  - Theater chase lights
  - Traffic lights
  - USO dance hall's jukebox

Material sources

Most of the animation materials you'll need are available from model railroad hobby sources. Slow-speed Hankscraft geared motors are sold under the brand names of Switchmaster and American Switch & Signal, although I've found similar motors in surplus stores and at hobby flea markets. The chain and sprockets are marketed by Grandt Line and industrial gear suppliers. Drive belts are available in video repair kits sold by electronic suppliers. K&S sells brass bars, rods, and tubing useful for bearings, shafts, and supports.

Dancers

Build a dance hall so its entire dance floor is a plastic disk that slowly rotates, with the dancing couples attached to it. The floor isn't seen by the viewer, so the movement produces

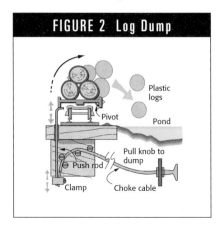

FIGURE 2 Log Dump

an illusion of dancing couples. To top it off, make an acrylic plastic jukebox and illuminate it through a rotating disk of multicolored lenses. This produces a jukebox with changing colors, while a tape player and concealed speaker provide appropriate dance music.

Log dump

Figure 2 shows the device that dumps logs off flatcars and into a pond filled with real water. Pulling an automobile choke cable lifts a brass rod to tip the flatcar deck and dump the logs.

The special flatcars were originally marketed by Cox (no longer in the model railroad business), but the same cars were also sold under the old AHM label. Although they're made for the toy market, the flatcars are detailed enough so a little paint and weathering does wonders. These cars come with three hollow plastic logs that float.

Log loading boom

Figure 3 shows the log boom that loads flatcars at the lumber camp. The spar pole is cut into two sections just below the boom. A brass bearing tube runs down through the fixed lower section and into the layout. A smaller-diameter brass rod is attached to the upper section so it extends down through the fixed lower portion. One motor, concealed under the bench

top, rotates the rod to shift the boom from side to side.

A second motor raises and lowers the counterweighted main cable, which comes up through a dummy donkey engine and over the pulleys on the boom. A pair of weighted dummy cables, one on each side, gives the illusion that the boom is being rotated by the donkey engine. Add a Märklin electromagnet, detailed with log jaws, to the main cable to handle the logs.

Kadee's plastic logs can easily be modified for magnetic pickup. Roll a 1"-wide strip of tin into a tube that fits snugly inside the log. Center the tin tube within the log, secure it with cyanoacrylate adhesive (CA), and cement the plastic ends in place. The magnet is strong enough to attract the tin through the thin log wall, while the log remains light enough to float in the pond.

Moving automobiles

Moving vehicles always capture attention. On the LP&T, a continuous loop of model airplane multi-strand control line cable runs in a thin slot built into the pavement. Small pins, silver-soldered to the metal cable at irregular intervals, extend above the slot to pull autos along the street.

Figure 4 shows a cross section of the street with cable slots fabricated from code 100 rail soldered to brass crossties. The thin gap between the

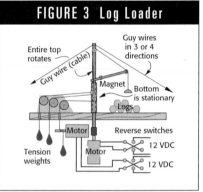

FIGURE 3 Log Loader

railheads allows the vertical pins to pass, but keeps the cable from lifting out of the slot. Soldering ⅛" lengths of 1/16" brass tubing to the cable at 12" intervals helps keep the cable within the slot.

Install heavy-duty, slow-speed motors with identical drive pulleys at both ends of the street. One motor and pulley set should be stationary; the other motor needs a spring-loaded mounting to maintain tension on the cable. Determine the cable loop's length, cut off the excess, and then silver-solder the splice for maximum strength.

Wiking automobiles, available from Walthers, work the best, as they have free-rolling axles. Drill a small hole into the plastic chassis just ahead of the front axle to fit over the cable pins. Test-run the device, make any necessary adjustments, and build the street surface.

Neon lights and signs

There are three ways of simulating the neon signs so common in the 1940s. For large signs on buildings, paint plastic letters with fluorescent colors that glow when illuminated by "black" or ultraviolet light. Unfortunately, there's no easy way to make the signs flash like many of the originals.

Neon store-window sign kits are made in numerous designs by Quality Products Co. and sold by Walthers. These signs are pieces of clear acrylic with the design and lettering engraved on the window's inside surface. The engraved areas are filled with colored dye and illuminated by a tiny lamp that shines into the window's edge. Some of these signs include flashers to create an excellent flashing neon effect. Similar ready-made neon signs are manufactured by Miniatronics.

Lighted jewelry provides another source of neon signs. One battery-operated brooch, about 1¾" tall, has a green palm tree with an orange trunk. Several other patterns are also available. A built-in switch allows either continuous or flashing operation. Mount the brooch into the side of a building and add appropriate lettering around it. On the LP&T, the brooch marks "The Green Palm Club," producing a night scene reminiscent of old gangster movies. This sign appears in the background of fig. 4.

Rotating fuel oil and water spouts for locomotives

Figure 5 shows an easy way to use a Hankscraft motor mounted beneath the track board to swing an oil or water spout over either service track. Use soft surgical tubing for the coupling so a locomotive can push the spout out of the way in case someone leaves it fouling the service track.

Sawmill equipment

Sawmills have lots of interesting action that can be animated as shown in fig. 6. Make a drag chain to pull logs from the pond into the mill from Andeco plastic chain and matching sprockets, available from Grandt Line. It's driven by a single Hankscraft motor. Attach small pins to the plastic chain so they catch and push the logs up into the sawmill. Once they're out of sight inside the mill, the logs can drop through a hole and into a collection box hidden beneath

the layout. The large circular saws may be simulated with a pair of Dremel saw blades mounted on belt-driven horizontal shafts and run by a single motor.

Use a Hankscraft motor to operate a slider-crank and spring-loaded cable to move the log carriage back and forth in front of the rotating saw blades. To complete the illusion, mount a partially cut log on the carriage so its flat side faces the blades.

Two matching loops of Andeco

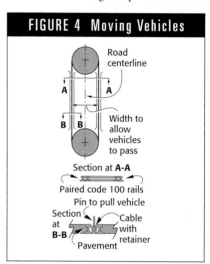

FIGURE 4 Moving Vehicles

Road centerline

Width to allow vehicles to pass

Section at A-A

Paired code 100 rails

Pin to pull vehicle

Cable with retainer

Pavement

chain, driven by a single motor, make an excellent miniature "green chain" for the sawmill. Tiny pins on the chains carry the freshly cut boards past the sorter, who grades and stacks them at the finishing end of the mill.

Action can also be added inside the conical sawdust burner by using flickering red and yellow lights. One of Radio Shack's pamphlets has a simple flicker circuit that uses a no. 555 timer chip. If you don't want to build one, GRS Micro-Liting makes a ready-to-use unit that is sold by Walthers.

An incense burner is another possibility, but I'd go easy on its use. A lot of dense smoke may be a fine visual effect for video or photo sessions, but it can get old in a hurry during operating sessions.

Scrap-metal loading crane

The crane loading scrap metal in fig. 7 requires a mechanism similar to the log loader. Mount the crane cab on a ³⁄₁₆″ brass tube that rotates in a telescoping tube bushing cemented into the layout. One Hankscraft motor rotates the cab with a belt drive, while two others raise and lower the boom and operate the hoist cable. Mount these two motors on the cab rotation tube so they turn with it to minimize cable problems.

A Märklin electromagnet handles the scrap metal. Simulate the baled steel scrap by gluing bits of tin to blocks of balsa wood. Then wrap the blocks in crushed aluminum foil. Once they're painted and weathered, the blocks look like crushed and baled automobiles.

Sunset and sunrise

To achieve the full benefit of special layout lighting effects, you'll want to dim the layout room lighting. Use incandescent lighting arranged in sev-

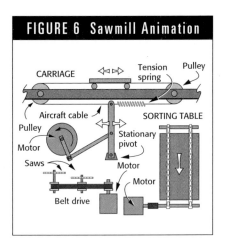

FIGURE 6 Sawmill Animation

eral circuits for 7-ampere lamp dimmers. They're available as dining-room dimmers at most large hardware stores. Since this involves potentially lethal 110-volt electrical power, get professional help for this step if you're not familiar with such work and the local electrical code.

Mount the dimmers next to each other with their control shafts geared together. Drive the setup with a slow-speed motor that takes several minutes for full rotation. For the sunset sequence, run the motor and turn the dimmers down until the room lights are almost extinguished. Use a limit switch to turn the motor off so the lamp filaments are left barely glowing. Then the motor can

FIGURE 5 Oil or Water Spout

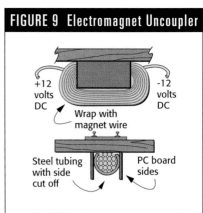

FIGURE 9 Electromagnet Uncoupler

+12 volts DC

-12 volts DC

Wrap with magnet wire

Steel tubing with side cut off

PC board sides

FIGURE 7 Scrap Loading Crane

Motors mounted on bracket attached to center tube

Epoxy center tube to cab

Rotation motor

Hoist motor

Belt drive

Boom motor

Bushing cemented to crane track, and benchtop

FIGURE 8 Two-color Traffic Signals

Red

Green

Red

Green

Light-emitting diodes

+5 volts DC
-5 volts DC

SP-DT microswitch with common normally open

C
NO
NC

1 RPM motor

To next set of signals

Cam

NC
NO
C

---

be reversed for a gradual sunrise. Turning the dimmer back on, if the filaments are completely off, defeats the gradual sunrise as the lamps will suddenly "snap" to partial brilliance.

Traffic lights

Two-color traffic lights use a combination of electrical and mechanical parts as shown in fig. 8. The signals are fabricated from K&S brass tubing and channel, with Radio Shack's smallest red and green light-emitting diodes (LEDs) for the lights. By connecting the LEDs as shown, the brass mast serves as one lead while a single insulated wire, passing up through the mast, completes the circuit. The red and green colors change by reversing the polarity of the DC voltage. Note that a current-limiting resistor is wired in series to control the LED's brilliance.

Use a thick plastic cam mounted on a Hankscraft motor to operate a single-pole double-throw (SPDT)

micro-switch that controls the traffic signals. The LP&T has six intersections with traffic lights, but any number can be wired in parallel or more SPDT switches can be added at random around the cam.

DC power for the traffic light LEDs comes from a pair of 5-volt, 300-milliampere battery eliminators, with the positive output of one connected to the negative output of the other, creating a bipolar ±5-volt DC supply. Connected as shown, the "C" output of each micro-switch is either +5 volts or -5 volts, changing as the cam rotates. This permits each intersection's traffic lights to be controlled by the output from a single microswitch.

Electromagnet uncouplers

Concealed electric uncouplers are handy on any layout equipped with Kadee Magne-Matic knuckle couplers. Figure 9 shows how to make a concealed electromagnet uncoupler that

can be controlled with a push button. This device has a 2"-long electromagnet that creates a strong magnetic field across the track. It really snaps the coupler knuckles open and easily shifts the coupler into the delayed uncoupling position once the couplers are separated.

Use a piece of 1" steel tubing with one side cut off to form the core. Attach a pair of side pieces, made of printed-circuit-board material, to the core. Wrap enameled magnet wire lengthwise around the core until it's filled. The wire size is a matter of choice; fine wire requires more turns and a higher DC operating voltage, but it uses less current.

Mount the coil so the cut edges of the steel core are just below the ties and rails. When it's actuated, the magnetic field will arch up and across the rails to open the coupler knuckles. Mark the center of the concealed uncoupler with a dab of paint on a tie.

Use a heavy-duty push button to control the coil, and connect a diode across the coil to suppress the voltage "kick" when the button is released. Don't use the small Radio Shack red push buttons: they aren't adequate for this application.

Animation is an opportunity that's just beginning to develop in the hobby of scale model railroading. Materials are readily available and the construction methods and mechanics are easy to master. Once you have experienced the added realism of scale animation, you'll be looking at nearly everything on your layout from a different perspective.

2

Build an Operating Tunnel Curtain

By Gary Hoover
Photos by the author

ADD A BIT OF DRAMA TO YOUR LAYOUT
WITH REALISTIC ANIMATION

This smoky old Alco demonstrates well the need for a
tunnel-ventilation system. Without it, the fumes would
linger, endangering the crew of the next train.

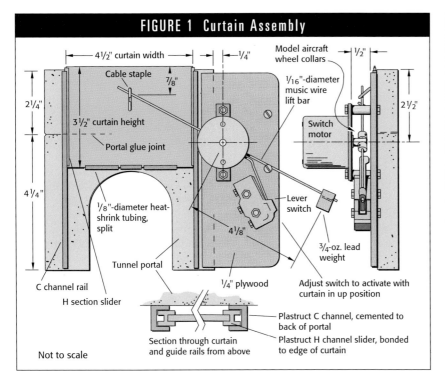

FIGURE 1 Curtain Assembly

- 4½" curtain width
- ¼"
- ½"
- Model aircraft wheel collars
- Cable staple
- ⅞"
- 2¼"
- 1/16"-diameter music wire lift bar
- 3½" curtain height
- Portal glue joint
- Switch motor
- 2½"
- 4¼"
- ⅛"-diameter heat-shrink tubing, split
- 4⅛"
- Lever switch
- Tunnel portal
- ¾-oz. lead weight
- C channel rail
- H section slider
- ¼" plywood
- Adjust switch to activate with curtain in up position
- Not to scale
- Plastruct C channel, cemented to back of portal
- Section through curtain and guide rails from above
- Plastruct H channel slider, bonded to edge of curtain

FIGURE 2 Portal

A | B | B
A

Cut on dashed lines
Discard shaded portions
Glue parts A and B together

Bill of Materials

A. I. M.
110-126 abutment wings (2)
110-128 poured concrete tunnel (2)

A-Line
166-13000 lead weight (.75 oz.)

Badger
165-16107 Accu-Flex Gloss White paint

Circuitron
800-5501 BD-1 block detector (2)

Con-Cor
222-9060 power substation

Du-Bro
596 3/32" aircraft wheel collars (2)

Evergreen
269-14250 V-groove siding

Great Glass
15009 Kelly-green glass stain

Oregon Rail Supply
538-114 two-light signal (includes LED and resistors R2 and R3)

Plastruct
C-4 C channel, ⅛" x .050"

Radio Shack
(D1) 275-214A relay, 12VDC (3)
(D1) 276-1144 diode (3)
(R1) 271-153A resistor, 1,000 ohm
(S1) 275-016 lever switch
(S1) 278-1215 22g wire

Switchmaster
(M1) 169J1001 switch motor

Walthers
934-703084 decal stripes, red

Miscellaneous
¼" x 3" x 7" plywood
⅛" diameter shrink tube
1/16" diameter music wire
mounting hardware
solder
wire-cable brad or brass strip

If you're looking for a way to add animation and drama to your tunnel portal scene, you might try borrowing a practice used by the Burlington Northern Railroad. I've visited Burlington Northern's Stevens Pass, cut through the rugged and beautiful Cascade mountains of northern Washington. There, the eight-mile-long Cascade Tunnel features a forced-air ventilation system that prevents train crews from being asphyxiated by diesel exhaust.

Powerful and deafening blowers on the east end of the tunnel draw in fresh air and force it out the west portal. To keep the fresh air flowing properly through the tunnel, a metal "curtain" is used to close the eastern end while the blowers are operating.

When a train approaches from either direction, the blowers shut down and the tunnel curtain rises, much like an automatic garage door, accompanied by a whoosh of air into the tunnel. After the train clears the tunnel, the curtain closes and the ventilation process begins all over again.

After seeing this dramatic operation on the BN, I quickly decided that my HO scale Missouri, Kansas & Quincy RR needed a similar tunnel curtain for its Wahsatch Tunnel. I spent the entire plane ride back home from Washington sketching the preliminary design for my operating HO scale version. I couldn't wait to get started!

The plan

I wanted my operating door to be absolutely reliable. The embarrassing thought of a train crashing through a stuck tunnel curtain during an NMRA open house passed through my mind more than once. Fortunately, a simple fail-safe electrical circuit keeps this from happening.

Another feature I wanted was fully automatic operation. The MKQ uses the Circuitron optical-detection system for its automatic signal system so I chose to use it also to detect trains approaching the tunnel and to open the curtain.

Finally, I wanted the MKQ's operating curtain to capture the drama and flavor of BN's Cascade Tunnel, though I wasn't interested in modeling an exact scale replica if I didn't have to. Since the MKQ is a free-lance railroad, I happily enjoy the luxury of doing that without inviting a nitpicker attack.

Draw the curtain

Figure 1 shows the dimensions and locations of the parts necessary to construct an operating tunnel curtain for a single track in HO scale. Figure 2 shows how to cut and glue the portals to obtain the height needed when the curtain is in the up position.

Cutting the plaster portal is easy with a sharp, wide razor saw. Work slowly and be sure to clean plaster from the blade often. I've found that a very light coat of Pam vegetable spray on the blade helps.

I joined the two portal halves with epoxy and let them dry on a flat, hard surface. The portal front and sides can be painted using your favorite technique. Don't paint the back of the portal because you'll need a good gluing surface for the curtain rails and the motor mount base.

I used a piece of V-grooved scribed Evergreen siding for the curtain, cutting the width first. For the curtain to operate smoothly, it must have a constant width.

The curtain was initially cut about twice as long as it would finally be. The initial extra length helps align the rails when they're bonded to the portal. I bonded a strip of Plastruct H section to each edge of the curtain to get a smooth sliding fit between the curtain and the rails. The H section rides inside the C channel rails glued to the portal.

The curtain also needs something to engage the lift bar, so I glued a wire-cable brad (used by electricians to affix wiring to joists) to the rear of the curtain with epoxy. A piece of brass strip could serve the same purpose.

Finally, I slit three short segments of heat-shrink tubing and cemented them to the bottom of the curtain for a soft cushion air seal. Paint and decal stripes finished this stage.

Another kind of rails

I treat portal rails just like track rails. They need to be straight, spaced properly, and free of glue, paint, and nicks. The first step in installing the rails was aligning the tunnel portal with the center line of the curtain or vice versa.

Next, I set the C-channel portal rails in place with a very slight gap remaining between them and the curtain edges. Finally, when everything was aligned, I tack-glued the top and bottom of each rail with a drop of cyanoacrylate adhesive (CA).

I gently slid the curtain up and down by hand to make sure every-

A slow-motion switch motor raises the curtain at a realistic speed.

thing was working correctly. It should travel up and down the track smoothly and by its own weight. If it doesn't, something is binding. For a finishing touch, I added a fillet of epoxy along the entire outer edge of each portal rail. As the epoxy set, I continued to check the curtain for proper operation.

Get the motor running

Since I wanted to capture the proto-typically slow operation of the curtain,

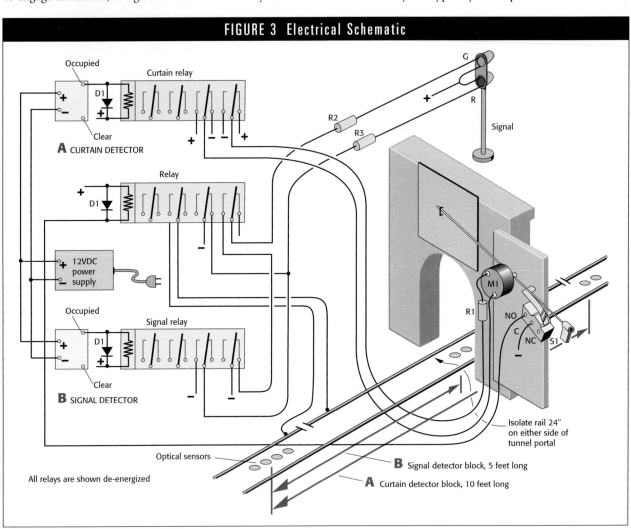

FIGURE 3 Electrical Schematic

Occupied
Curtain relay
D1
+ −
Clear
A CURTAIN DETECTOR

Relay
+
D1

12VDC power supply

Occupied
Signal relay
+
D1
+
Clear
B SIGNAL DETECTOR

All relays are shown de-energized

G
+
R2
R3
R
Signal

M1
R1
NO
C
NC
S1

Isolate rail 24" on either side of tunnel portal

Optical sensors

B Signal detector block, 5 feet long
A Curtain detector block, 10 feet long

a Switchmaster switch motor was a natural choice. I mounted it to a piece of ¼" plywood that I glued to the back side of the portal with more epoxy.

I added .75 ounces of lead to the free end of the throw bar to help balance the tunnel curtain's weight. Without this weight, the curtain traveled too fast going down and too slow going up.

Next, I connected the motor to a temporary 12V DC power supply to test the operation.

Blower house

I used a great deal of "modeler's license" when I built the blower house and air intake. The main walls of the blower house were made from A.I.M. tapered abutment wings while the remainder of the surrounding structures were simple, quick, and fun mini-scratchbuilding projects.

I needed a source of power for the tunnel's massive air blowers. If you think your electric bill was high last summer, imagine what BN's Cascade Tunnel must suck up yearly! Similar to the BN operation, the MKQ has a power substation near the blower house. I built the power substation from a Con-Cor kit, but due to space limitations I used only half of the kit.

By the way, a neat method of representing those glass insulators found on power poles and transformers is to first paint the insulators white and then apply one or two coats of colored-glass stain available at most craft stores. The result is shiny, glassy-looking insulators.

The fail-safe device

Figure 3 shows how the electrical system is connected. I used two Circuitron optical-detector blocks; one for triggering the tunnel-curtain operation and the other for triggering the signal at the face of the portal. The signal-detection block overlaps the tunnel-curtain detection block.

The two-aspect signal at the tunnel portal provides important information to the train crew. The signal is normally red when the curtain is down and will only display green if the curtain is fully up and no other trains are in the signal-detection block. This interlocking feature between the curtain position and the signal-detection block was easily

Here's the completed curtain in its closed position. The blower house for tunnel ventilation is just for show, but your visitors don't have to know that.

accomplished by routing the power through relays.

The fail-safe feature uses the position of the curtain to either apply or cut power to a short section of isolated rail on either side of the portal. When the curtain is up, a small lever switch closes and provides power to the track. If for some reason the curtain fails to open completely, the locomotive will stop on the dead section of track before it hits the curtain.

I soldered a 1,000-ohm, 1-watt resistor to the Switchmaster motor in series for realistic curtain operating speed. You may need to vary the value

of this resistor for your particular application. If your curtain travels too slowly, try a slightly lower value resistor and vice versa.

It works!

I had fun designing and building the tunnel curtain, but the real fun lies in the operation. I especially enjoy watching first-time visitors when they spot the closed tunnel curtain with a train approaching. To their amazement, the curtain slowly rises just before the train arrives. At the same time, the red signal winks to green. It's a bit of fun that never gets old.

3

Build a Working Coal Tipple

By Jim Ferenc
Photos by the author

PVC PIPE, A 1″ AUGER BIT, AND A
WINDSHIELD-WIPER MOTOR ARE THE KEY INGREDIENTS

With the Hecla Mine tipple looming above, the crew of the Louisville Turn relays signals to No. 909's engineer as they load their last string of hoppers at Hecla Mine.

Automation at Hecla Mine

I model the Colorado & Southern Ry.'s Northern Division (standard gauge) in HO scale. My layout is fairly small—13 feet by 16 feet—so I've been concentrating on animation to increase its play value during operations.

Rocky Mountain Fuel Co.'s Hecla Mine is a major source of activity on the C&S Northern Division. The focal point of the mine is the operating tipple that can load a string of 50-ton hoppers or gondolas with real black diamonds in about 10 seconds per car. The mechanism is an improved version of a design described by Rick Spano in the July 1979 *Railroad Model Craftsman*.

The parts are standard hardware store items, with some styrene and brass from the hobby shop. The only exotic component is a windshield wiper motor. The mechanism fits inside the crusher/tipple structure, which has a removable roof for easy loading of the coal hopper. The coal it dispenses is real—I crush coal and sift it through a common kitchen strainer.

The tipple mechanism is a coal bin that gravity feeds an auger-style drill bit which carries the coal out to the gate over the track, as shown in fig. 1. The bin holds 22 carloads of coal, more than enough for an operating session. The motor-driven auger moves the coal about 3″ from the bin to the waiting gate and acts as a valve, stopping the flow of coal when it isn't turning.

A motor for motion

The heart of the mechanism is a windshield wiper motor. I liberated mine from a '73 Subaru at an auto junkyard. Other automotive motors like those for power windows should also work as they have the necessary torque to drive the auger and crush any coal that might jam the mechanism. As you browse the junkyard for your motor, select one that includes a metal mounting plate.

My wiper motor has two speeds, as most do, and an electrical connector with several spade lugs. To find which lug runs the motor at each speed, connect one lead of a 12-volt, DC power supply to the motor body and the other lead to one of the spade lugs. Locate the lug which runs the motor at slow speed, and also note the polarity needed to run it counterclockwise. My motor draws about 1 amp at low speed.

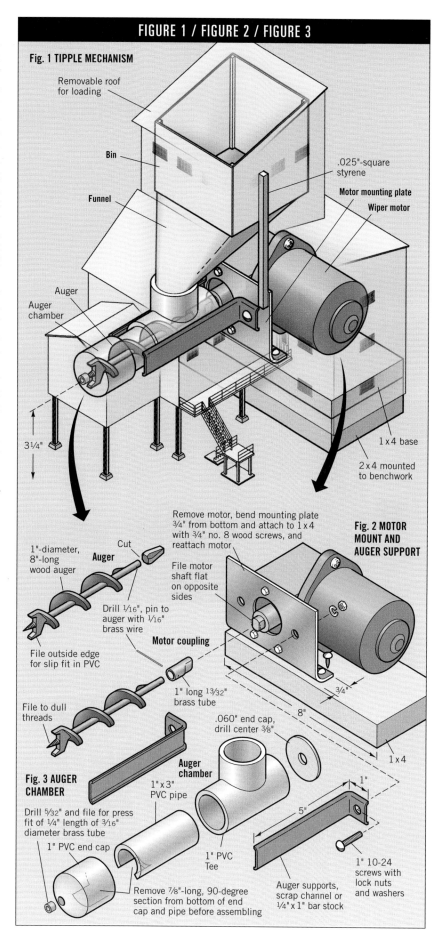

FIGURE 1 / FIGURE 2 / FIGURE 3

Fig. 1 TIPPLE MECHANISM

Removable roof for loading

Bin

Funnel

Auger

Auger chamber

.025"-square styrene

Motor mounting plate

Wiper motor

3¼"

1 x 4 base

2 x 4 mounted to benchwork

Remove motor, bend mounting plate ¾" from bottom and attach to 1 x 4 with ¾" no. 8 wood screws, and reattach motor

Fig. 2 MOTOR MOUNT AND AUGER SUPPORT

File motor shaft flat on opposite sides

Motor coupling

1"-diameter, 8"-long wood auger

Auger

Cut

Drill ¹⁄₁₆", pin to auger with ¹⁄₁₆" brass wire

File outside edge for slip fit in PVC

File to dull threads

1" long ¹³⁄₃₂" brass tube

¾"

8"

1 x 4

.060" end cap, drill center ⅜"

1"

5"

Fig. 3 AUGER CHAMBER

Drill ⁵⁄₃₂" and file for press fit of ¼" length of ³⁄₁₆" diameter brass tube

1" PVC end cap

1" x 3" PVC pipe

Auger chamber

1" PVC Tee

Remove ⅞"-long, 90-degree section from bottom of end cap and pipe before assembling

Auger supports, scrap channel or ¼" x 1" bar stock

1" 10-24 screws with lock nuts and washers

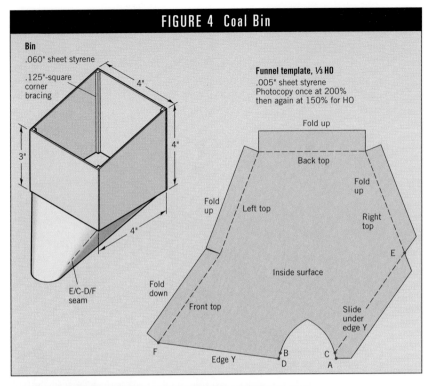

FIGURE 4 Coal Bin

Bin
.060" sheet styrene

.125"-square corner bracing

3"

4"

4"

4"

E/C-D/F seam

Funnel template, ⅓ HO
.005" sheet styrene
Photocopy once at 200%
then again at 150% for HO

Fold up

Back top

Fold up

Left top

Right top

Fold up

E

Inside surface

Fold down

Front top

Slide under edge Y

F

Edge Y

B
D

C
A

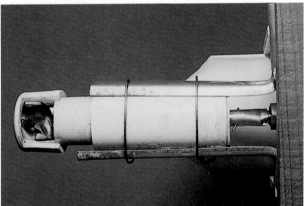

Fig. 5 AUGER CHAMBER. This bottom view shows how the tip of the auger rests in the brass bearing in the end cap, the brass tube coupling to the motor shaft, and the wires clamping the chamber to the auger supports.

Construction

Your motor will probably differ from mine, so use my mounting (fig. 2), only as a suggestion. I was able to bend the bottom of my motor's mounting plate (with the motor removed) to form a bracket. You may need to bolt yours to a piece of angle. I made my support from a salvaged garden hose hanger, but the drawing shows how to use brass or aluminum bar stock.

As shown in fig. 3, I made the auger chamber from 1" PVC pipe and components. I aligned the outlet openings in the pipe and end cap opposite to the stem of the tee and used five-minute epoxy to assemble the parts.

The auger is a 1"-diameter, 8"-long, wood auger drill bit—the cheapest I could find. I cut off the square tang with a hacksaw and dulled the screw point with a file. I also lightly filed the outside of the cutting edge of the auger for a slip fit into the 1" pipe.

As an end bearing for the auger, I used a piece of ³⁄₁₆" brass tube in the end cap. I drilled a ⁵⁄₃₂" hole and carefully enlarged it with a round jeweler's file until I could just press the tubing in. After inserting the auger into the chamber with its tip firmly in the end-cap bearing, epoxy the endplate in place. Then pin the motor coupling to the shank of the drill, as shown in fig. 5.

The dimensions I used for the auger chamber keep a full turn of the auger's blade in front of and behind the stem of the tee; this prevents coal moving through the tipple when the auger is stopped. To move the coal forward, the auger rotates counterclockwise (opposite to its normal drilling motion), which also keeps the screw threads on the tip of the auger from drilling out the bearing in the end cap.

Assembly

Slide the auger chamber between the support bars and slip the coupling over the motor shaft, pinching down the coupling around the motor shaft with needlenose pliers. While holding the auger chamber against the motor shaft, bind it tightly to the support bars with 9" lengths of 14-gauge solid copper wire in front of and behind the tee fitting. Twist the wire with pliers to tighten. This ensures that the auger coupling will not move away and uncouple from the motor shaft. I made 1" loops of twisted wire (in case I'd want to undo it later) and clipped off the rest, as seen in fig. 1.

The bin

The coal bin shown in fig. 4 is sized to hold more coal than all of the cars to be loaded in one operating session. In HO scale, a 50-ton hopper holds about a quarter cup of coal, which is about 4 cubic inches. The bin holds 48 cubic inches and the funnel another 40 cubic inches, so I can load about 22 cars.

The funnel template is one-third size for HO; you can enlarge it on a photocopier to meet your needs. I made the funnel from .005" styrene sheet. Slide side E/C under edge Y until the dotted edge X ends up under edge Y and points A, C, and E line up under points B, D, and F, respectively.

Hold the funnel in shape and slip it into the bin and cement the tabs to the inside edges. Now cement the seam along edges X and Y. The funnel opening should be about ¾" in diameter—enlarge it if necessary. If there are any gaps in your bin and funnel fill them with five-minute epoxy.

Completing the mechanism

The completed assembly is shown in fig. 6. Position the funnel opening inside the PVC tee. Ensure that the bin is vertical, then cement .250"-square styrene strips to the sides of the bin, and fasten them to the motor baseplate using epoxy. Seal the funnel/tee joint with a bead of five-minute epoxy.

I use a 12-volt, 2-amp, DC power

supply wired to a push-button switch (Radio Shack part no. 275-618) in my layout fascia to control the tipple.

I screwed and glued an 8"-long 2 x 4 to my benchwork so that when the tipple mechanism is on it, the center of the auger is 3¼" above the railhead. To adjust the centering over the track, I placed a hopper on the mine spur and briefly ran coal through the tipple. I slid the mechanism back and forth until the coal discharged in the center of the car, then screwed it to the 2 x 4.

The tipple

I covered my mechanism with a tipple made of corrugated sheet styrene. Figure 7 provides a general sketch of my design. Of course, as long as it covers the mechanism you can make yours in any shape and as large as you want.

Fig. 6 OVERALL ASSEMBLY. Here's the completed mechanism for the working tipple. The 1 x 4 will be screwed to a 2 x 4 that's permanently attached to the benchwork. The painted area on the bin was visible through the windows, and this neutral color let it blend in.

FIGURE 7 Tipple Housing, ½ N

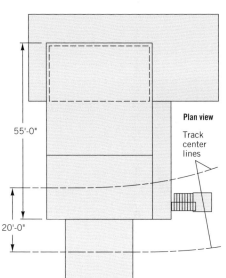

Plan view

Track center lines

55'-0"

20'-0"

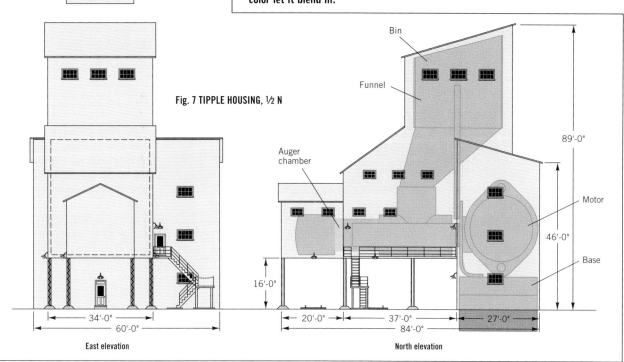

Fig. 7 TIPPLE HOUSING, ½ N

Bin

Funnel

Auger chamber

Motor

Base

89'-0"

46'-0"

16'-0"

34'-0"

60'-0"

East elevation

20'-0"   37'-0"   27'-0"

84'-0"

North elevation

An Operating Windmill

By Rodger Gredvig
Photos by the author

AN ANIMATED DEVICE FOR N AND HO SCALES

Providing motion to an otherwise static scene, the author's scratchbuilt windmill appears to be pumping water for an adjacent railroad water tank.

Everyone enjoys animated scenes on a model railroad. For many of us this fascination began with Lionel and other toy trains that had smoking locomotives, log dumping cars, rolling oil barrels, operating highway crossing gates, and rockets launched from freight cars.

I've always found such action fascinating, and in an effort to create a little action on my Ntrak module I decided to see if I could develop a simple working windmill. My "pilot model" was suitable for HO, but after that I was able to make a smaller version that looks good in N scale.

Pilot model

For my first attempt I used parts from Campbell HO kit no. 1604. I discarded the kit's tower and constructed a smaller structure from Plastruct A-3 ³⁄₃₂" angles, with .030"-square styrene strip for the diagonal bracing.

I filed down the cast ring located about midway out on the fan blades to reduce its bulk. Next I filed down the drive shaft to allow free movement of the fan, and cut down the size of the vane. Position the fan on the drive shaft, and carefully form a small mushroom-shaped cap on the shaft end with a soldering iron. Make certain that the fan spins freely.

Final version

The HO conversion was a bit large for N so I developed a much smaller version from some spoked sequin

Fig. 2. This view shows the two versions of the fan assembly. On the right, the one with the reworked Campbell kit fan works better, but it's a bit large for N scale. The one at the left uses spoked sequins.

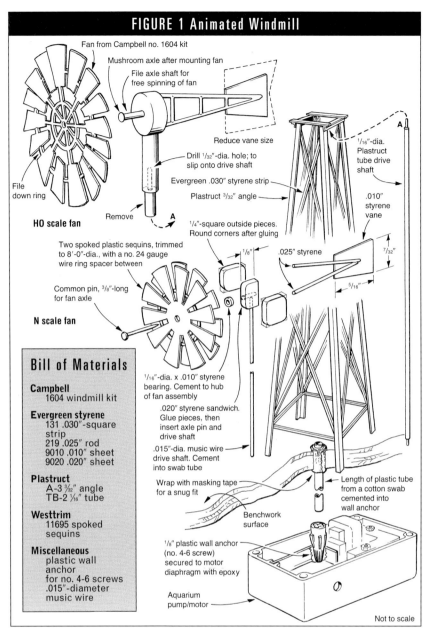

FIGURE 1 Animated Windmill

Fan from Campbell no. 1604 kit

Mushroom axle after mounting fan

File axle shaft for free spinning of fan

Reduce vane size

File down ring

Remove

HO scale fan

Drill ¹/₃₂"-dia. hole; to slip onto drive shaft

Evergreen .030" styrene strip

Plastruct ³/₃₂" angle

¹/₄"-square outside pieces. Round corners after gluing

Two spoked plastic sequins, trimmed to 8'-0"-dia., with a no. 24 gauge wire ring spacer between

Common pin, ³/₈"-long for fan axle

N scale fan

¹/₁₆"-dia. x .010" styrene bearing. Cement to hub of fan assembly

.020" styrene sandwich. Glue pieces, then insert axle pin and drive shaft

.015"-dia. music wire drive shaft. Cement into swab tube

Wrap with masking tape for a snug fit

Benchwork surface

¹/₁₆"-dia. Plastruct tube drive shaft

.010" styrene vane

.025" styrene

⅛"

⁷/₃₂"

⁵/₁₆"

Length of plastic tube from a cotton swab cemented into wall anchor

⅛" plastic wall anchor (no. 4-6 screw) secured to motor diaphragm with epoxy

Aquarium pump/motor

Not to scale

Bill of Materials

Campbell
1604 windmill kit

Evergreen styrene
131 .030"-square strip
219 .025" rod
9010 .010" sheet
9020 .020" sheet

Plastruct
A-3 ³/₃₂" angle
TB-2 ¹/₁₆" tube

Westtrim
11695 spoked sequins

Miscellaneous
plastic wall anchor for no. 4-6 screws
.015"-diameter music wire

material. I trimmed the blades on two sequins to make them a scale 8'-0" in diameter and fastened them as an overlay separated by a wire ring, with the blades staggered. The ring was made by wrapping 24-gauge copper wire around a AAA battery. Because of its light mass this model doesn't operate as smoothly as the Campbell one; still, its proportions are better for N scale.

For the fan shaft I used a straight pin cemented into a simulated gearbox housing (made with layers of .020" styrene that were cut and filed to shape). The construction of the gearbox and the directional vane is shown in fig. 1. Fashion and cement a .062"-diameter circle of .010" styrene to the fan as a bearing hub.

I considered making a more delicate tower using .025"-diameter styrene rod. However, the sturdy nature of the original design used with the Campbell fan proved to be the best choice for the windmill on my traveling Ntrak module.

Drive unit

After discovering that vibration will cause the fan to spin, I developed a suitable drive system using an aquarium pump. Cut a length of plastic tube from a cotton swab and wrap a few turns around it. Drill a hole in the layout base to provide a snug fit around the tape. Attach a small plastic wall anchor to the pump diaphragm with epoxy, as shown in fig. l. The pump is mounted under the layout with wood screws, separated from the wood by rubber grommets to reduce vibration, and centered under the hole drilled in the plywood base.

The drive shaft to the fan assembly is a length of ¹/₁₆" Plastruct tube

(actually a tube with a wire center) with the top end trimmed as shown in fig. 1 and cemented into the fan gear housing. Press-fit it into the small wall anchor at the bottom. Drill out the platform opening at the top of the tower to ³/₁₆" diameter. The drive shaft must not touch the tower structure anywhere, or it will shake the tower to pieces.

The windmill must also point in certain directions, determined by experimentation, to get the proper harmonics to make the fan spin. Otherwise you'll get a lot of chattering, and the assembly will vibrate without the fan rotating.

I wired a 110-volt dimmer switch into the pump line to slow the pump motor, smooth out the oscillation,

and reduce chattering. An on/off switch in the front profile board of my Ntrak module gives visitors an opportunity to get involved.

WARNING: Readers unfamiliar with electrical safety precautions should not make the 110-volt connections. These must be made properly to avoid the possibility of a dangerous, potentially fatal electric shock.

Finally, I painted the model, using silver for the entire structure and adding some grimy black color around the gear housing. You may want to apply a few touches of rust and some general weathering. Now you have an animated attraction to fascinate yet another generation of impressionable modelers.

Build a Slow-Motion Crossing Gate Drive

By Brad E. Smith
Photos by the author

THE TORTOISE SWITCH MOTOR LENDS REALISTIC ACTION

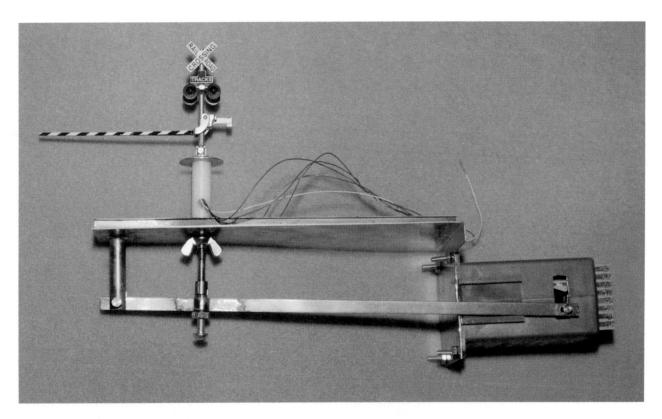

Realistic operating crossing gates have been a personal dream since I began building my HO scale New Haven RR. I started with a pair of Tomar's beautiful no. 863 crossing signals with gates. These gates take about 18 seconds to move in either direction, so they're much too slow compared to prototype gates which cycle in about 6 seconds. My "bullet-proof" gate mechanism is designed to correct this timing problem.

Circuitron's Tortoise switch machine is a reliable actuating device that takes 3 seconds to cycle at 12

volts. By reducing its operating voltage to 7 volts, the cycle time lengthens to about 5 seconds—a good compromise for model gates.

The drawing shows the simple lever system I devised to convert the switch machine's movement into an adjustable vertical motion.

Tools and materials

The K&S Engineering metal display at your local hobby shop or hardware store contains most of the necessary materials. The 4-40 tap is also available at hardware stores.

Working with brass isn't difficult and it's fun if you use the right tools. For this project, you'll need sheet metal cutting pliers, a hacksaw, a propane torch, rosin-core solder, paste soldering flux, and a razor saw.

Sheet metal bracket

Lay out the main bracket on .032 sheet brass using a scriber to mark the outline, center line, and hole locations shown in the bracket template. Cut it out using the sheet metal cutters, but be careful of the sharp edges. If your cutting ripples an edge, hammer it down against a flat piece of steel.

You'll need an actuator beneath each gate, but it doesn't have to be perpendicular to the crossing. Both plates can be bent the same way, or one gate can have a left-hand mechanism and one a right-hand. The only difference is the direction you bend the motor mount.

Align the bend line even with the top of the jaws and clamp the brass plate in a vise. Make a sharp 90-degree angle by tapping the bend with a hammer. Position the Tortoise on the bracket, mark the mounting screw locations through the flange openings, and drill all the holes.

Channel braces

Two braces made of K&S channel must be soldered across the top of the bracket. The work has to be clean, so sand the surfaces to be soldered with new sandpaper until all oxidation is gone. Don't touch the cleaned areas as the oils on your skin will repel the solder.

Coat the mating surfaces with paste flux and position the channels so you can solder both in one heating of the bracket. Cut 12 pieces of solder about an inch long and place them against the channels at the joint. As the brass gets hot the solder will melt and be drawn into the joint by capillary action.

Installing the clevis

The clevis post is made from ⁵⁄₁₆"-diameter brass rod. First mark and drill the horizontal hole through the end of the rod. It's much easier to start the drill bit properly if you center punch the location.

Cut the slot perpendicular to the hole with a hacksaw as shown in the drawing. Trim the rod to the proper length and file the end square. Drill the end of the post to accept a short piece of ⅛"-diameter brass rod to serve as a locating pin. Clean the surfaces, apply flux, and assemble. Turn the bracket upside down, heat the clevis and bracket, and apply solder until it flows evenly around the base of the post.

Operating lever

The operating lever is made from a .032" x ¼" brass bar. I soldered a brass lug to the lever and drilled and tapped it for an optional set screw

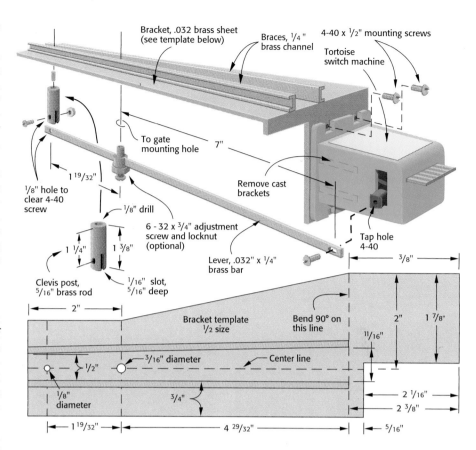

and lock nut that's handy for tweaking the final gate adjustment.

The actuating lever travels in an arc, so a slot is required to link it to the straight motion of the Tortoise throw arm. Drill a couple of holes first and then finish shaping the opening with a round jeweler's file. Tap the hole in the throw arm for a 4-40 screw. Don't use a lubricant when tapping plastic.

Installation

Assemble the mechanism and mount the crossing gate. Add a 470-ohm, ½-watt resistor in series with each Tortoise motor to reduce 12 volts DC to the desired 7 volts. Support the motor end of the mechanism with an L-shaped bracket made of scrap brass or wood.

A thin piece of piano wire may be used to operate other brands of gates. Drill a loose-fitting hole through the side of the actuating lever in place of my adjustment screw. Make a 90-degree bend about ½" from the end of the piano wire. Pass the long end up through the gate mounting hole, slip the short end through the lever, and bend the wire down to secure it. Mount the actuator so the piano wire can move freely through a small hole in the layout to operate the gate.

Bill of Materials

Circuitron
6000 Tortoise switch machine

K&S Engineering
127 ⅛" brass rod
133 ⁵⁄₁₆" brass rod
185 ¼" brass channel
240 .032" x ¼" brass strip
253 .032" x ¼" x 10" brass sheet

Tomar
863 crossing signal with gate

Miscellaneous
4-40 x ½" right-hand machine screws 4-40 nuts
6-32 x ¾" right-hand machine screws 6-32 nuts

I used a Dallee no. 553 infrared optical detection circuit to sense trains approaching the crossing. This circuit has three sets of infrared detectors which work perfectly for a two-track main line.

A Dallee no. 587 grade crossing controller with an electronic bell operates the lights and gates through a no. 555 relay. These circuits have been operating for several months without problems.

Build a Three-Position Semaphore Mechanism

By Gary Hoover

ADD PROTOTYPICAL ANIMATION TO YOUR RAILROAD'S OPERATION

Left: The semaphore displays a "clear" aspect for this eastbound ATSF yellowbonnet approaching Oak Grove, Illinois, on the Missouri, Kansas & Quincy Railroad. Middle: With the train in the home block, the semaphore displays an "occupied" aspect. Right: The signal remains in the "approach" position until the last car clears the distant block.

The operating semaphore signals on my Missouri, Kansas & Quincy Railroad always attract lots of attention from visitors. Onlookers stare in amazement as the semaphore blade, powered by a slow-motion motor, slowly moves to the "occupied" position as the train enters the home block. Then, after then train has completely passed through the home block, the blade slowly rises back to the "clear" position. Most of the semaphores on my railroad operate in this two-position fashion. However, real semaphores can also move to a third position that is often referred to as an "approach" indication. For the "approach" position, the semaphore's blade is halfway between

vertical and horizontal. This position signifies to the engineer that he must begin slowing down his train and expect to make a stop at the next signal. I wanted some of my semaphores be able to operate in three positions, so I designed a device that would do the job. The simple, reliable, and inexpensive mechanism described in this article has been in operation on the MKQ since 1994 and continues to provide interesting prototypical animation.

Principle of operation

My three-position semaphores are normally in the vertical, or "clear," position if no trains are present in the home and distant blocks. The "home"

block is the block of track the semaphore is in and the "distant" block is the block of track just beyond the home block. When the train enters the home block, the semaphore blade lowers to the horizontal, or "occupied," position. The blade stays in this position as long as any portion of the train is in the home block. When the last car of the train passes out of the home block and into the distant block, the blade rises to the "approach" position. As long as any portion of the train is in the distant block, the blade displays "approach." Finally, when the last car of the train exits the distant block, the blade moves back to the original "clear" position. When a train comes from the opposite direction by entering the distant block first, the semaphore reverts to a two-position signal. The blade moves from "clear" to "occupied" as the locomotive passes from the distant block into the home block and remains in the "occupied" position until the entire train has passed through the home block.

The mechanism for the three-position semaphore is actually the device I use for my two-position semaphores but with an additional slow-motion motor installed to establish the "approach" position of the blade. As with the two-position semaphores, the motor that connects directly to the semaphore blade operates in response to the electronic block occupancy detector in the home block. The second motor operates in response to the detector in the distance block. The lever arm on the distant block's motor is simply used as a blocking device to keep the lever arm on the home block's motor from returning to the "clear" position when the train passes out of the home block. Since Switchmaster motors are designed to stall out without burning up, no harm is done by stopping them at any position, even though electrical power remains applied to the motor.

Building the mechanism

It is simplest if the mechanism is mounted on a separate base made from plywood or pine. This allows most of the construction work to be done at the workbench rather than under the layout. After the mechanism is complete, it is a simple matter to mount the base to the layout's framework and hook up the throwrod for the semaphore blade.

The parts I used to construct the mechanism are listed in the bill of materials and can be found in almost any hobby shop. I tried to keep the design functional and easy to construct and adjust. If you are handy with cutting and bending metal, you might want to simplify the construction of the angle assemblies by making them from one piece of sheet brass. My metalworking capabilities are limited, so I opted for the construction techniques that required only simple cutting using common hand tools.

First, mount the motors (part no. 6) on the wooden base with the center lines of the shafts 3¹¹⁄₁₆" apart. Clock-

Fig. 1 The semaphore is shown in the "clear" position, which means no trains are present in either the home block or the distant block. The motor for the home block is on the left and is connected to the semaphore. The distant block motor is on the right.

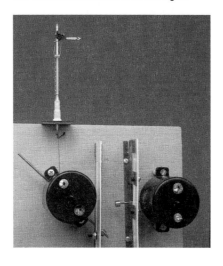

Fig. 3 The lever arm on the distant block motor rotates counterclockwise as soon as the locomotive enters the distant block. The semaphore blade still shows "occupied," since some of the train is still in the home block.

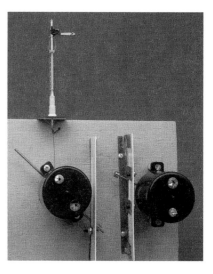

Fig. 2 When the train enters the home block, the semaphore lowers to the "occupied" position.

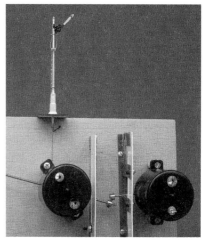

Fig. 4 When the last car of the train passes out of the home block, the home block motor will try to return to the "clear" position but is stopped by the distant block's lever arm. This establishes the "approach" position for the semaphore blade. When the last car of the train passes out of the distant block, both lever arms return to the clear position shown in fig. 1.

ing of the motors isn't really critical as long as the lever arms can travel through their required arcs without hitting the mounting standoffs. The mounting standoffs supplied with the motors should be ¹³⁄₁₆" long. Install the lever arms (part no. 7) and use an aircraft wheel collar (part no. 9) on each side of the motor shaft to keep the arm in position. I found that the mechanism works best if the distance from the motor shaft to the collar on the end of the lever arm for the home block's motor is slightly longer than that for the distant block's motor. The

shorter shaft-to-arm length on the distant block's motor assures that the home block's lever arm stops solidly when moving from the occupied to the approach position.

The angle assemblies that mount between the two motors are fabricated next. They provide a guide slot for the lever arm (part no. 7) to travel in so that the arms don't ride up and over each other. Also, the angle

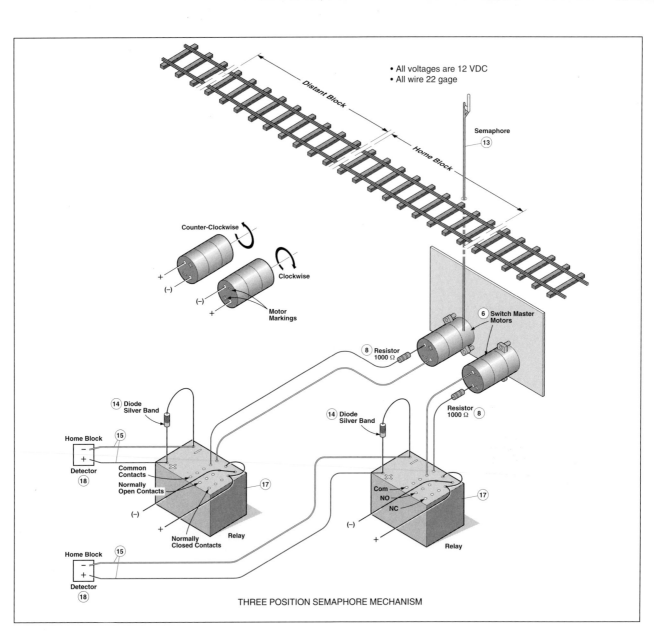

• All voltages are 12 VDC
• All wire 22 gage

Distant Block

Home Block

Semaphore (13)

Counter-Clockwise

Clockwise

(−) +

(−) +

Motor Markings

(6) Switch Master Motors

(8) Resistor 1000 Ω

Resistor (8) 1000 Ω

(14) Diode Silver Band

(14) Diode Silver Band

Home Block (15)

− +

Detector (18)

Common Contacts
Normally Open Contacts

(−)

+

Normally Closed Contacts

Relay

(17)

Com
NO
NC

(−)

+

Relay

(17)

Home Block (15)

− +

Detector (18)

THREE POSITION SEMAPHORE MECHANISM

Bill of Materials

Part No. Item	Description/Quantity	Size	Manufacturer/ Item number
1	Brass angle (2)	¼" x ¼" x 4¾"	K&S no. 175
2	Brass strip (2)	½" x .025" x 4¾"	K&S no. 236
3	Brass strip—upright (2)	½" x .025" x 1¼"	K&S no. 236
4	Styrene guide strip (2)	4¾" x 1" x .060"	Evergreen no. 9060
5	Brass strip—stop (2)	½" x .025" x 1¼"	K&S no. 236
6	Slow-motion motor (2)	—	Switchmaster
7	Wire-lever arm (2)	³⁄₃₂" x 4"	K&S no. 506 music wire
8	Resistor (2)	1000-ohm, 1-watt	Radio Shack no. 271-153
9	Wheel collars (7)	³⁄₃₂" I.D.	Dubro no. 138
10	Screw/washer (3)	4-40 x ¼"	Carl Goldberg no. 502
11	Nut (3)	4-40 self-lock	Dubro no. 170
12	Screw (4)	no. 4 x ½"	Carl Goldberg no. 568
13	Semaphore (1)	—	Tomar no. 853 or no. 854
14	Diode (2)	1 amp, 50 PIV	Radio Shack no. 275-214
15	Wire (1 roll)	22 gauge solid	Radio Shack no. 278-1215
16	Solder (1 roll)	60/40 rosin core	Radio Shack no. 64-005
17	Relay (2)	12-volt DC2	Radio Shack no. 275-214
18	Block detector (2)	—	Circuitron no. BD-1

Fig. 5 The end view of the mechanism. The home block motor is on the left and the distant block motor is on the right. Aircraft wheel collars hold the lever arms and semaphore blade wire in the correct position.

Fig. 6 Adjustable stops make setting the semaphore blade positions quick, easy, and precise.

place it over the motor's lever arm on the side opposite from the angle assemblies. An aircraft wheel collar placed outside of the wire will keep it in the correct position. Leave a small gap between the wheel collar and the wire so that the wire is free to pivot slightly rather than bend when the lever arm travels through its arc.

Adjusting the mechanism

Adjustment is fast and precise by simply positioning the stops correctly and then tightening the lock bolts. It helps to solicit the aid of a friend who can call out the position of the semaphore blade as you adjust and lock down the stops. Start with the semaphore's blade in the "clear" position. Adjust the distant block's upper stop so that its lever arm just touches the home block's lever arm. Next, move the home block's lever arm down to where the blade is in the "occupied" position. Move the stop up to where it is just touching the home block's lever arm and tighten the lock bolt. Finally, move the home block's lever arm to where the semaphore blade indicates "approach." Move the distant block's lever arm down until it just contacts the home block's lever arm and then set and lock the distant block's lower stop. The course adjustment for the mechanism is now complete. Once the mechanism is wired and running on its own, a final fine-tuning of the stops will probably be necessary to get the blade positions exactly correct. Once the final adjustments are made, you can expect years of trouble-free operation.

Wiring and detection

The wiring for the three-position semaphore is easy to do and uses common items available from any electronics supply store. For detection, I used Circuitron's BD1 optical system, but any detector circuit that can power a 12-volt DC relay will work fine. The relay simply switches polarity to the motor; the motor then runs either clockwise or counterclockwise. To make the motor run at the speed I like, I use a 1000-ohm, 1-watt resistor rather than the 1200-ohm resistor furnished with the motor.

You may want to experiment with different resistor values until your blade operates at the speed you like best. If your motor runs too fast, try a

assemblies serve as a mounting surface for the adjustable stops (part no. 5). The stops make setting the "clear," "occupied," and "approach" blade positions quick, easy, and precise. Construction of the angle assemblies involves cutting some brass angle (part no. 1), brass strips (parts nos. 2, 3, and 5) and styrene strips (part no. 4) to the correct size. I used a hacksaw and vise to cut the brass angle and tin snips to cut the brass strip. Then I soldered together the angle (part no. 1) and the brass strips (parts nos. 2 and 3) strips. The top edge of the completed angle assemblies should just fit under the installed lever arms. I cut the styrene guide strips (part no. 4) to size using an X-acto knife. Using styrene for the guide strips rather

than brass makes cutting the inside slot easier. I drilled two ⅛"-diameter holes to form the ends of the slot and then cut the rest out using an X-acto knife and straightedge.

After cutting the guide strips, attach them to the upright strips (part no. 3) using super glue. Position the guide strip just enough above the top of the angle assembly to allow free movement of the 3⁄32"-diameter lever arm. Finally, secure the completed angle assemblies to the wooden mounting base with small screws (part no. 12).

Now install the mechanism assembly beneath the layout and make the semaphore connection. Bend the end of the thin wire going up to the semaphore blade into a small closed loop;

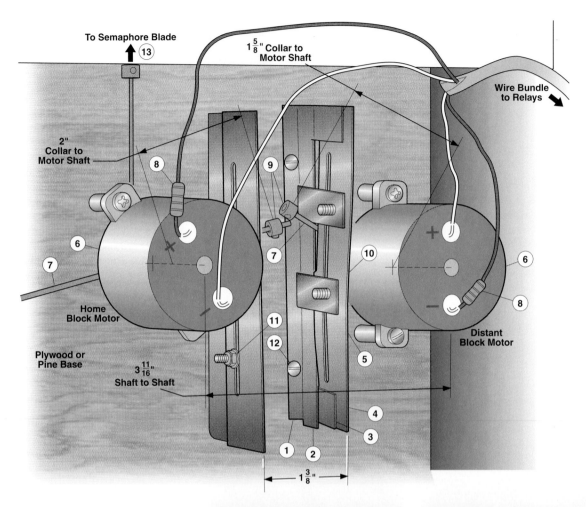

To Semaphore Blade — (13)

$1\frac{5}{8}$" Collar to Motor Shaft

Wire Bundle to Relays

2" Collar to Motor Shaft

(8) (9)

(6) (7)

(7)

(10)

Home Block Motor

(11)

(12)

Plywood or Pine Base

$3\frac{11}{16}$" Shaft to Shaft

Distant Block Motor

(6)

(8)

(5)

(4)

(3)

(1) (2)

$1\frac{3}{8}$"

slightly higher ohm value like 1100 or 1200 ohms. If the motor runs too slow, use a lesser ohm value such as 900 ohms. Also, note the polarity markings "+" and "-" on the back of the motor. If you hook your power supply up as shown in the wiring diagram, everything should work fine. If for some reason the motor runs the wrong way, simply reverse the wires at the motor.

Note the diode added across the two poles of the relay that connect the relay to the block detector. This diode keeps electrical spikes in the relay's coil from damaging the delicate electronics in the block detector. To keep from having a dead short, make sure the end of the diode with the silver band is connected to the positive (+) lead coming from the block detector.

Soldering the wires to the pins on the relay is simple if you follow a few guidelines. I use a small, 30-watt "pencil" soldering iron and thin 60/40 electronic solder. Pre-tin both the pins and the wire with solder.

Fig. 7 The lever arms travel in slots so that they don't ride up and over each other.

Fig. 8 Top view of the home block motor showing the semaphore connection to the lever. A small gap between the aircraft wheel collars on each side of the wire allows the wire to pivot rather than bend when the lever travels through its arc.

Then, while holding the wire with a pair of small needlenose pliers, place the wire against the pin and touch the tip of the soldering iron to the joint. When the solder melts, remove the iron and hold the assembled joint for a few seconds until the solder hardens.

I think you'll enjoy operating your railroad with three-position semaphores. The animation provided by the semaphore along with the prototypical three positions will make the short time needed to construct the mechanism well worth it.

7

Amaze Your Friends with a Working Wig-Wag

By Woody Langley
Photos by the author

BUILDING A BRASS MAGNETIC FLAGMAN IN HO SCALE

Two old-timers watch a "Big Red" car near a crossing on the author's HO layout. The sound and motion of the wig-wag signal warn motorists.

This signal on the Eureka Southern is still wagging after all these years. Looks like the target has gotten bent. This signal is mounted atop a relay case, as was frequently done.

With the dawn of the 20th century, there came a revolution in transportation as Americans rapidly converted from horses to automobiles. Horses had always been pretty good at looking out for themselves, but the same couldn't be said for motorists. The old "Watch out for the trains" signs were no longer sufficient to protect railroad crossings, so flagmen, flashing lights, and warning bells were introduced.

The wig-wag is born

One device, developed by J. B. Hunt of southern California's Pacific Electric Ry., was an electromechanical hybrid of all three of these methods. The PE called it an "automatic flagman"; the more popular name was "wig-wag."

Between 1910 and 1920, the PE placed 117 automatic flagmen in service. These early versions were powered by electric motors, but excessive maintenance costs prompted an ingenious redesign. The motorized mechanism was replaced by an offset pair of electromagnets that alternately attracted an iron bar attached to the target shaft. With far fewer moving parts, there was less to wear out or break.

As of 1921 the PE had replaced all its original automatic flagmen with

Here's a finished wig-wag. How about those beautiful graphics that end up under the layout?

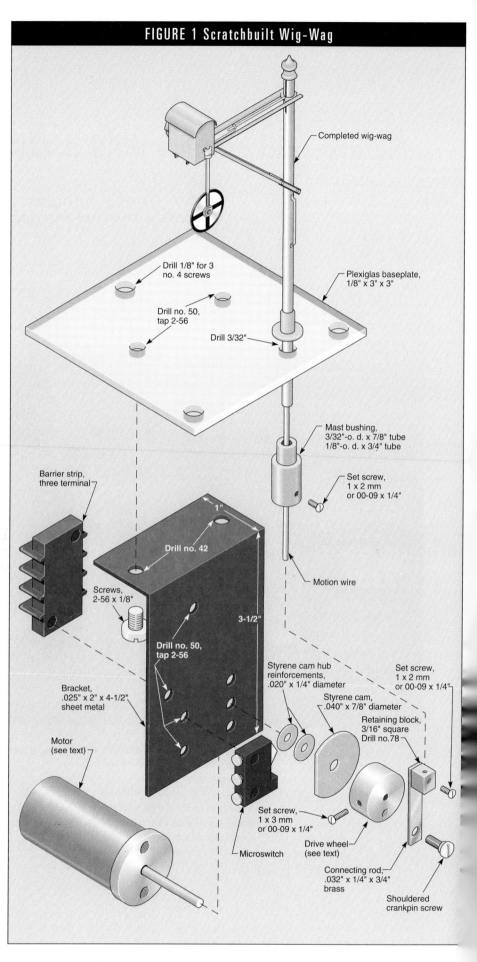

FIGURE 1 Scratchbuilt Wig-Wag

- Completed wig-wag
- Drill 1/8" for 3 no. 4 screws
- Drill no. 50, tap 2-56
- Drill 3/32"
- Plexiglas baseplate, 1/8" x 3" x 3"
- Mast bushing, 3/32"-o. d. x 7/8" tube 1/8"-o. d. x 3/4" tube
- Set screw, 1 x 2 mm or 00-09 x 1/4"
- Motion wire
- Barrier strip, three terminal
- Drill no. 42
- Screws, 2-56 x 1/8"
- Drill no. 50, tap 2-56
- Bracket, .025" x 2" x 4-1/2" sheet metal
- Motor (see text)
- Microswitch
- Set screw, 1 x 3 mm or 00-09 x 1/4"
- Styrene cam hub reinforcements, .020" x 1/4" diameter
- Styrene cam, .040" x 7/8" diameter
- Drive wheel (see text)
- Retaining block, 3/16" square Drill no.78
- Set screw, 1 x 2 mm or 00-09 x 1/4"
- Connecting rod; .032" x 1/4" x 3/4" brass
- Shouldered crankpin screw

FIGURE 2 Signal Drive

FIGURE 4 Motor Wiring

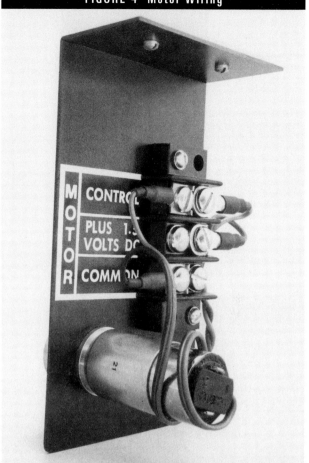

FIGURE 3 Switch Cam

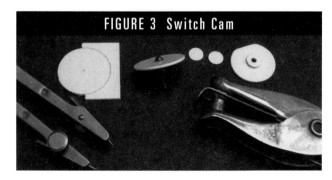

FIGURE 5 Motion Wire

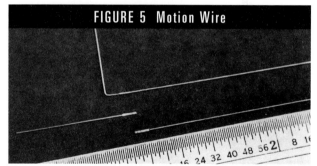

Fig. 2. A drivewheel and crank, hidden under the layout, make the wig-wag do its thing. The mechanism works like the drive rod on a steam locomotive.

Fig. 3. Below, left to right: To make a cam the author used dividers to scribe a circle in styrene, then snapped it out. He chucked it in his motor tool to turn it against a file and round it. Then he punched out the hubs with a paper punch.

Fig. 4. Here's the reverse side of the mechanism, showing the motor and barrier strip. Using lugs makes for neat wiring.

Fig. 5. Below is a completed motion wire. The portion that's hidden in the mast is .015″ wire; the visible part is .012″ wire. As shown with the unassembled parts, the author filed flats at the ends of each wire to make a strong joint; then he soldered them together.

electromagnetic models. By late 1926 about 500 of these were operating throughout the system, with more coming.

Bearing the trademark "Magnetic Flagman," these signals were manufactured by the Magnetic Signal Co. of Los Angeles. Not only were they used by the Pacific Electric, but other customers were the Atchison, Topeka & Santa Fe, the Southern Pacific, and other lines across the United States and Canada.

Wig-wags have been a hardy breed, a testament to their elegantly simple, yet sound, design. Although no longer legal for new installations, a few remain in operation today, enduring sentinels to warn motorists as they have done for most of this century.

The motor and microswitch

Scratchbuilding a working HO scale wig-wag isn't difficult, though it does require fabricating small parts from brass and soldering them together. I used a resistance soldering rig, but you'll do just fine with a conventional soldering iron. Figure 1 is a drawing of the model signal in its entirety.

To power my wig-wag I chose a Faulhaber micromotor with a slip-on reduction gear head. These motors sell for about $40 each and are imported by Micro Mo Electronics. They can be ordered through hobby shops or by mail from Foothill Model Works, P. O. Box 470, Willits, CA 95490.

A less expensive option would be the 24-volt DC motor with a 40:1 gearbox (part no. 60910) that's available from Micro-Mark, 340 Snyder Ave., Berkeley Heights, NJ 07922-1595, for $7.95. This motor will give a prototypical 42-rpm speed at about 4 volts.

Start by making a mounting bracket and attaching the motor to it, as shown in fig. 2. A homemade cam, mounted on the motor's drive shaft, engages a microswitch that won't allow the motor to stop running until the signal's target is hanging straight down.

Figure 3 shows how I used draftsman's dividers to make the cam from .040″ sheet styrene. My cam measures ⅞″ in diameter, but that measurement isn't critical. The two reinforcement disks were added to increase the hub's grip on the motor shaft. I made these by drilling center holes in .020″ styrene, then punching out the disks with a ¼″ paper punch.

Press the cam on the shaft, then mount the microswitch. These are available at electronics stores. Two good ones for this project are the Cherry E63 or the GC Electronics 35-822. You want the cam just close enough so the switch clicks during the transitions between round and flat areas.

Next, mount the electrical barrier strip on the opposite side of the bracket. As shown in fig. 4, I labeled my barrier-strip terminals COMMON, PLUS, and CONTROL. COMMON is the negative output from the power supply, PLUS is a straight-through positive output, and CONTROL is a second positive output interrupted by a switch.

Wire the motor leads to the COMMON and CONTROL terminals on the barrier strip. Connect one

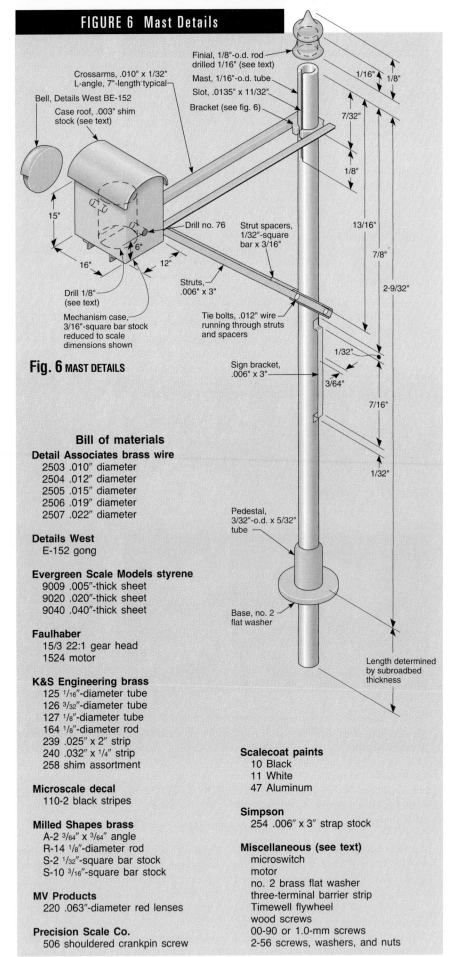

FIGURE 6 Mast Details

Finial, 1/8″-o.d. rod drilled 1/16″ (see text)
Crossarms, .010″ x 1/32″ L-angle, 7″-length typical
Mast, 1/16″-o.d. tube
Slot, .0135″ x 11/32″
Bell, Details West BE-152
Case roof, .003″ shim stock (see text)
Bracket (see fig. 6)
1/16″ 1/8″
7/32″
1/8″
15″
Drill no. 76
Strut spacers, 1/32″-square bar x 3/16″
13/16″
6″
7/8″
16″ 12″
2-9/32″
Drill 1/8″ (see text)
Struts, .006″ x 3″
Mechanism case, 3/16″-square bar stock reduced to scale dimensions shown
Tie bolts, .012″ wire running through struts and spacers
1/32″
3/64″
Sign bracket, .006″ x 3″
7/16″

Fig. 6 MAST DETAILS

1/32″

Pedestal, 3/32″-o.d. x 5/32″ tube

Base, no. 2 flat washer

Length determined by subroadbed thickness

Bill of materials
Detail Associates brass wire
2503 .010″ diameter
2504 .012″ diameter
2505 .015″ diameter
2506 .019″ diameter
2507 .022″ diameter

Details West
E-152 gong

Evergreen Scale Models styrene
9009 .005″-thick sheet
9020 .020″-thick sheet
9040 .040″-thick sheet

Faulhaber
15/3 22:1 gear head
1524 motor

K&S Engineering brass
125 1/16″-diameter tube
126 3/32″-diameter tube
127 1/8″-diameter tube
164 1/8″-diameter rod
239 .025″ x 2″ strip
240 .032″ x 1/4″ strip
258 shim assortment

Microscale decal
110-2 black stripes

Milled Shapes brass
A-2 3/64″ x 3/64″ angle
R-14 1/8″-diameter rod
S-2 1/32″-square bar stock
S-10 3/16″-square bar stock

MV Products
220 .063″-diameter red lenses

Precision Scale Co.
506 shouldered crankpin screw

Scalecoat paints
10 Black
11 White
47 Aluminum

Simpson
254 .006″ x 3″ strap stock

Miscellaneous (see text)
microswitch
motor
no. 2 brass flat washer
three-terminal barrier strip
Timewell flywheel
wood screws
00-90 or 1.0-mm screws
2-56 screws, washers, and nuts

FIGURE 7 Crossarm Bracket

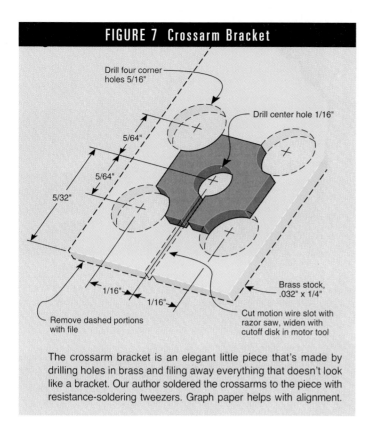

Drill four corner holes 5/16"

Drill center hole 1/16"

5/64"

5/64"

5/32"

1/16"

1/16"

Remove dashed portions with file

Brass stock, .032" x 1/4"

Cut motion wire slot with razor saw, widen with cutoff disk in motor tool

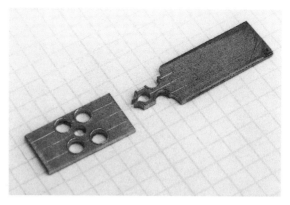

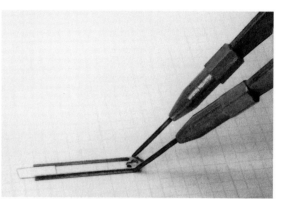

The crossarm bracket is an elegant little piece that's made by drilling holes in brass and filing away everything that doesn't look like a bracket. Our author soldered the crossarms to the piece with resistance-soldering tweezers. Graph paper helps with alignment.

wire from PLUS to the COMMON (C) terminal on the micro-switch and another wire from CONTROL to the normally open (NO) terminal.

Test the unit under power. The motor should run continuously with voltage applied to COMMON and CONTROL. Applying voltage to COMMON and PLUS should cause the motor to stop whenever the microswitch lever and flat spot on the cam coincide.

The drive mechanism

Next, add the drive wheel to the motor shaft. I used a Timewell no. 120 brass flywheel and drilled it to accept a crankpin screw. See fig. 1.

This crankpin is offset 9 scale inches from the center of the flywheel's bore.

Then came the brass connecting rod, drilled at one end to rotate freely on the crankpin screw shoulder. At the other end goes a brass retaining block. Drill the holes required in 3/16"-square bar stock before cutting this piece free and soldering it to the connecting rod.

Press the drive wheel onto the motor shaft with the crankpin screw opposite the cam's flat spot.

Make the baseplate and mount the motor bracket to it. My baseplate is a 3"-square piece of 1/8" Plexiglas. With the connecting rod full up or full down, drill a 3/32" hole in the baseplate

directly above the retaining block hole. Make the shouldered sleeve bushing that will retain the signal mast, and align the motion wire.

Make the motion wire. Mine is shown in fig. 5. For the sake of better appearance, I used lighter wire for the part of the motion wire that would be visible.

Building the signal

To determine the height of the signal mast, first measure the distance from where the base of the mast will sit—usually at railhead level or slightly below—to the underside of the subroadbed. In my situation this is exactly 1". To this measurement add the length of the retaining bushing (7/8") plus a scale 16'-6". Then cut a section of 1/16" tube to that total length.

Cut an 11/32"-long slot in one end of the mast tube. I used a Dremel no. 406 circular saw blade to cut a .010-wide swath that I widened to .0135" with a no. 80 drill bit in a motor tool. I pierced along the slot at intervals and carefully moved the bit back and forth like a milling cutter. Since this blade is no longer sold, an alternative would be a no. 409 abrasive disk. Its .025" width won't look as good, but operation won't be affected.

Next, cut the two crossarms to

FIGURE 8 Soldering Crossarms

Fig. 8. Wood blocks were used throughout the project for tacking down pieces to be soldered. Such simple homemade aids are the key to achieving accuracy.

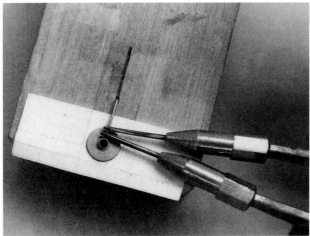

length. See fig. 6. Mine are 6 feet long. Southern Pacific drawings show 7-foot arms, but prototype photos that I've seen show some as short as 4 feet. It depended on the situation.

I made my crossarms from a supply of Milled Shapes .010″ x ⅟₃₂″ L-angle I laid in some years ago; I've learned, however, that this size (A-1) has been discontinued. The smallest size now available is ³⁄₆₄″ (A-2). You can use that and file each flange down to ⅟₃₂″ wide.

Next make the crossarm bracket as shown in fig. 7 and solder the cross-arms to it.

Make a mechanism case to the dimensions shown in fig. 6. It's easiest to file the roof contour and drill the holes before cutting the case off the end of your ³⁄₁₆″-square brass stock. To form the roof roll .003″ shim stock between the shank of a ⁷⁄₃₂″ drill and your fingertip. Solder the shim stock to the case, then use a sanding block, pulling down, to reduce the overhang to a scale inch all around.

Solder the mechanism case to the crossarms by pinning the components to a wood block as shown in fig. 8.

Unpin the assembly and slide the bracket down over the mast, adjusting it so that 9 scale inches of slot extend below the crossarm bracket. Solder it to the mast.

Make the cantilever support struts, also shown in fig. 6. To make sure they're identical, bond them together with cyanoacrylate adhesive (CA) before drilling the holes. A little heat from your soldering iron will break them apart again, or you can soak them in acetone.

Solder the spacers to the struts and test-fit them. File the spacers until the

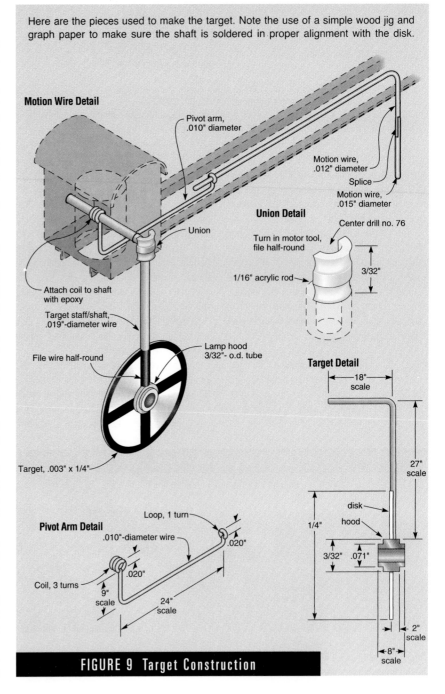

Here are the pieces used to make the target. Note the use of a simple wood jig and graph paper to make sure the shaft is soldered in proper alignment with the disk.

Motion Wire Detail

Pivot arm, .010″ diameter

Motion wire, .012″ diameter

Splice

Motion wire, .015″ diameter

Union

Attach coil to shaft with epoxy

Target staff/shaft, .019″-diameter wire

File wire half-round

Lamp hood 3/32″- o.d. tube

Target, .003″ x 1/4″

Union Detail

Center drill no. 76

Turn in motor tool, file half-round

1/16″ acrylic rod

3/32″

Target Detail

18″ scale

27″ scale

disk

hood

1/4″

3/32″   .071″

2″ scale

8″ scale

Pivot Arm Detail

Loop, 1 turn

.010″-diameter wire

.020″

.020″

Coil, 3 turns

9″ scale

24″ scale

FIGURE 9 Target Construction

struts come out parallel when positioned on the mast. Insert the pins that join the struts, then solder them and clip them off close to represent bolt heads. Make sure the struts are properly positioned, and solder them to the crossarms and mast.

Add the sign bracket and the pedestal. Position the base a scale 16'-6" from the top of the mast and solder. Turn the finial from brass rod. Test-fit but don't solder it to the mast, or it'll be in the way when you install the control rod.

You could turn a bell from brass rod. Instead, I modified a Details West gong casting by removing the bolt flange detail from around the perimeter and filing off the rear mounting stud. Then I cemented it to the case with epoxy.

Making the target

Figure 9 shows the parts that make up the target. To make the flat disk I first used a pair of dividers to impress a center hole in a piece of .003" shim brass. Then I lightly scribed a ¼"-diameter circle. I enlarged the hole with a ³⁄₃₂" bit, lined up the scribed circle with the hole in my paper punch, and stamped it out.

Next came the lens hood. I made mine by chucking a piece of ³⁄₃₂" brass tube in my motor tool and turning the piece out with files.

To assemble the target I slid the finished hood onto a length of ¹⁄₁₆" tube and tacked it with a drop of CA. I worked the target disk onto the flange until it was centered and perpendicular, then I soldered it. Soaking the assembly in acetone dissolved the CA so I could remove the piece of ¹⁄₁₆" tube.

Next came the target shaft, filed flat on one end and soldered to the disk. Last came the union.

Painting

Figure 10 shows the parts ready for painting. I first dry-etched the assemblies with aluminum oxide grit in a Paasche Air Eraser to provide good tooth for paint adhesion. I masked off the horizontal portion of the target shaft with hookup wire insulation, as well as the vertical portion of the motion wire. Then I airbrushed all the parts with Scalecoat Aluminum, going back over the target and staff with White.

To mask off the 1"-wide black ring

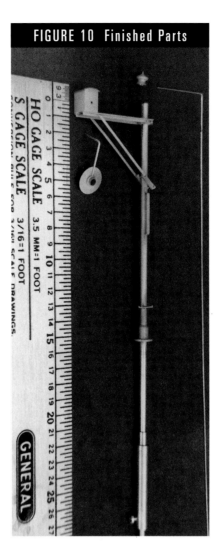

FIGURE 10 Finished Parts

Fig. 10. The parts of the wig-wag are ready for painting. Woody has etched them with a miniature sand blaster.

around the edge of the target, I used thin styrene circles, as shown in fig. 11. The cross stripes were added with decals and sealed with a clear finish.

Details and calibration

A 2"-long plug is needed to properly space the red lenses in the target hoods. I made mine by inserting 2" of a short length of ¹⁄₁₆" tube into a length of ³⁄₃₂" tube and tacking with a drop of CA. Sand the exposed portion of the ¹⁄₁₆" tube on a disk sander until it's flush with the larger tube. Soak the parts in acetone, and extract the plug. Center the 2"-long plug inside the hood tube, then put in the lenses and secure them with Walthers Goo.

Form the pivot arm as shown in fig. 9, then assemble the target shaft to the mechanism housing. Do this at the workbench—installation on the layout comes later.

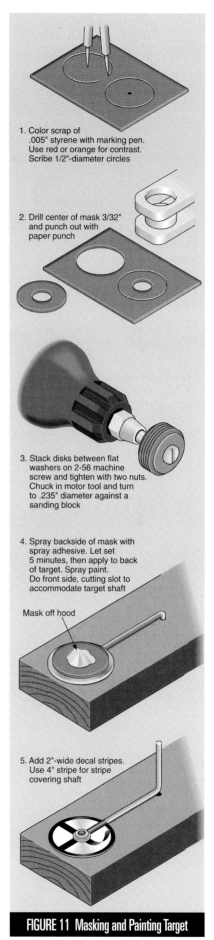

1. Color scrap of .005" styrene with marking pen. Use red or orange for contrast. Scribe 1/2"-diameter circles

2. Drill center of mask 3/32" and punch out with paper punch

3. Stack disks between flat washers on 2-56 machine screw and tighten with two nuts. Chuck in motor tool and turn to .235" diameter against a sanding block

4. Spray backside of mask with spray adhesive. Let set 5 minutes, then apply to back of target. Spray paint. Do front side, cutting slot to accommodate target shaft

Mask off hood

5. Add 2"-wide decal stripes. Use 4" stripe for stripe covering shaft

FIGURE 11 Masking and Painting Target

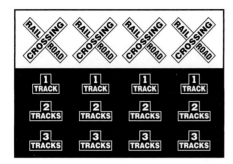

Insert the motion wire into the mast, and trim the horizontal leg so it clears the mechanism case. Check that the wire is parallel to the crossarms, bending it if necessary. Rotate the target to its extreme left position, and snip off the end of the motion wire just shy of the loop. Bend the motion wire enough to engage it in the loop.

Next, lower the signal mast into the baseplate bushing while feeding the .015″ leg of the motion wire through the hole in the connecting-rod block. Lock the mast with the bushing set screw.

Turn the drive wheel so its crankpin is at either 3 or 9 o'clock, and snug down the connecting-rod block. Turning the drive wheel by hand, run the motion wire to its highest and lowest extremities. It should extend a scale 9″ above and below the center of the crossarms. If not, loosen the set screw and adjust accordingly.

Again turning the drive wheel manually, observe the target. It should describe equal arcs to the left and right. If it doesn't, bend the pivot arm slightly to adjust it.

Operate the signal under power to test the stopping action of the micro-switch. If the target doesn't come to rest straight down, adjust the relationship between the flat spot on the cam and the drive wheel crankpin by twisting the cam on the motor shaft.

Now laminate the RAILROAD CROSSING and TRACKS signs to .005″ styrene with spray adhesive, and fasten them to the mast bracket with five-minute epoxy.

Installation on the layout

Drill a no. 52 hole through the layout 13 feet from the near rail and sufficiently to the right of the road-way so the target doesn't swing out beyond the curb line. Remove the signal from the bushing, and substitute a short length of ¹⁄₁₆″ tube protruding ¼″ above the baseplate. Key this tube into the layout hole from underneath. Drill three starter holes for wood screws, and secure the baseplate. Remove the ¹⁄₁₆″ tube, and try inserting the signal from the top of the layout. If the mast binds, enlarge the subroadbed hole to ⁵⁄₆₄″ or larger until the mast slips easily into the bushing.

Connect the barrier strip to your power source. My own signals are powered by a GRS CIL-125 LitePac and controlled by a Circuitron DT-2 detection unit and ER-1 relay with the BR-2 bell ringer added for some sound effects.

And there you have it. Your model motormen can worry a little less about autos suddenly materializing in front of them, and your motorists will be safer too. And you'll have had the fun of building a marvelous little bit of railroad history.

8

Go Fly a Kite! (or an Airplane)

By Rick Spano

TWO EASY PROJECTS
FOR ADDING ACTION
TO YOUR LAYOUT

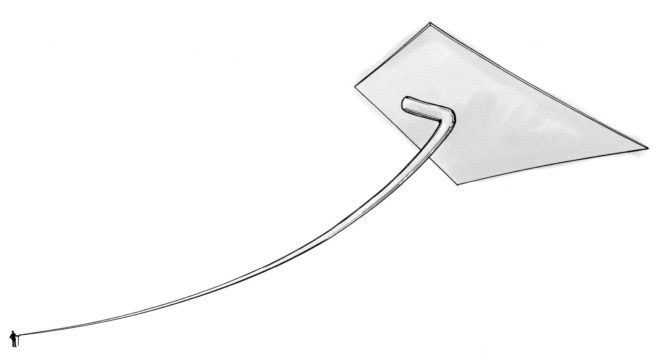

As a child I was fascinated watching the animated watchman snap in and out of the gatehouse as a train passed. Both Lionel and American Flyer had a version of this accessory. As much as this image remains fondly in my memory, though, it's not the type of animation I would like now on my layout—the action is too quick and unrealistic.

Oh, I would love to see a miniature gateman walk out and shine his lantern near the tracks as a model train approaches, but because of the technical difficulties I doubt that a realistic animated HO or N scale walking person will be produced in my lifetime. There are lots of other model situations that lend themselves to fairly realistic animations, though, like a boy flying a kite and a man flying a control-line model airplane.

Go fly a kite!

A person flying a kite is one of the easiest forms of animation to accomplish. The kite appears to be floating in the air, but in reality is supported by a curved wire.

To animate the kite I use a small fan mounted in the ceiling. This causes the kite to bob and weave in a somewhat periodic fashion. The viewer himself modifies this pattern of motion unwittingly, as shown in fig. 1, when he places himself between the fan and the kite. As he shifts position he changes the air pattern reaching the kite.

If you don't want to depend on visitors to modify the kite's flying pattern, use either an oscillating fan or a slowly rotating, irregularly shaped pattern blocking the wind stream, as shown in fig. 2.

And as long as we're talking fans, how about using them to animate windmills or rustle clothes hanging on a wash line?

FIGURE 1

Observer randomly programs movement of the kite by changing the pattern of air currents

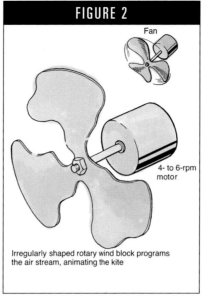

FIGURE 2

Irregularly shaped rotary wind block programs the air stream, animating the kite

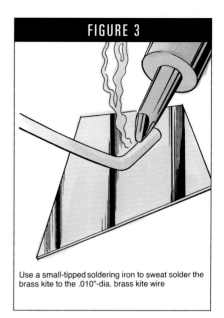

FIGURE 3

Use a small-tipped soldering iron to sweat solder the brass kite to the .010″-dia. brass kite wire

Kite construction

Picking the correct wire size is the most crucial part of constructing the kite. For my N scale kite I used a 7½″ length of Detail Associates .010″ brass wire, yielding a string 100 scale feet long. If you would like an 80- to 100-foot string in HO scale, try Detail Associates .015″ wire. For S and O, try K&S .015″ music wire.

Curve the wire by pulling it through the thumb and forefinger of your right hand while slowly rotating it away from your left.

You could make the kite from paper and cement it to the wire, but I have found that method too flimsy. Instead I cut the kite from .002″ brass shim stock and tin it lightly with solder on one side. Then I tin the last ¹⁄₁₆″ of the wire and solder the kite to it. See fig. 3.

You can either cement the other end of the wire to the figure's hand or bend the end of the wire, thread it through a hole drilled in the hand, and fix it in a hole in the ground, as shown in fig. 4.

The airplane

Obviously, a miniature man standing on the end of a rotating gear motor shaft does not entirely mimic his real-life counterpart—his feet don't move! This fact, though, is hardly noticeable one foot from the edge of the layout in N scale and two feet from the edge of the layout in HO.

The most difficult part of this animated scene is the airplane itself. In devising a means of fabricating such a tiny model, I remembered the advice of modelers who built fine detail

parts for their brass locomotives: "If you can see it and hold it, you can build it." After some thought, I came up with this procedure.

Place a 3″ x 3″ sheet of .002″ brass on a hard, smooth surface such as steel or glass. Lay a steel ruler on the brass close to the edge, and scribe along the edge of the ruler with a no. 10 X-acto blade until the blade cuts through. Remove and discard this strip of brass.

Move the rule .03″ from the newly cut edge, and cut off a parallel strip to be saved. Now cut a strip .025″ wide. These two strips will become the wings and horizontal stabilizers respectively.

Carefully lay these out on a smooth scrap piece of pine .035″ apart and parallel to each other. Secure the ends

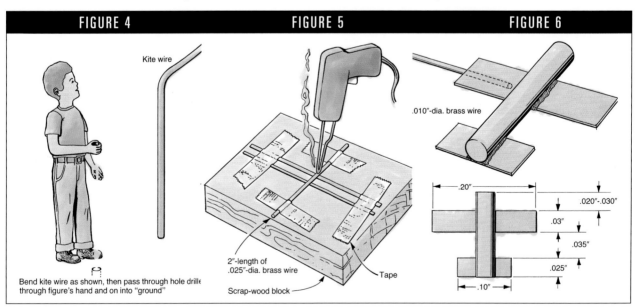

FIGURE 4

Kite wire

Bend kite wire as shown, then pass through hole drilled through figure's hand and on into "ground"

FIGURE 5

2″-length of .025″-dia. brass wire

Scrap-wood block

Tape

FIGURE 6

.010″-dia. brass wire

.20″

.10″

.020″-.030″

.03″

.035″

.025″

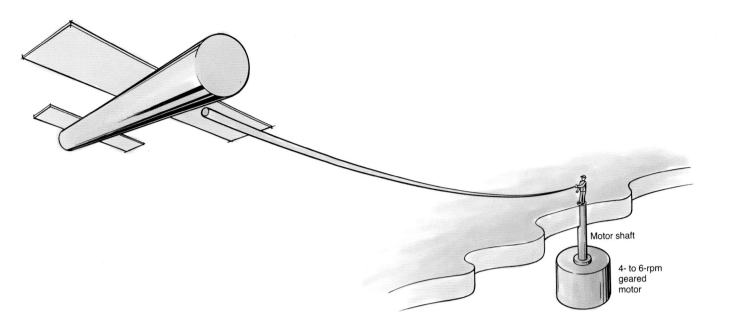

Motor shaft

4- to 6-rpm geared motor

with tape, and lightly tin the centers for about ¼″ length.

Next tin about an inch of a 2″ length of .025″-diameter brass rod. Lay the rod perpendicular to the two strips and solder it (see fig. 5). This is your fuselage.

Cut off the left wing ³⁄₃₂″ from the center of the rod, but don't cut off the right wing just yet. Tin about the last ¼″ of a piece of .010″ brass wire 4″ long. Then slide it under the left wing almost to the .025″-diameter wire. This is the tether that will go from the plane's wing to the man's hand. See fig. 6.

Now it's true that two lines are

actually used to control such a plane, but in N scale this discrepancy is hardly noticed. In scales larger than HO, solder two wires to the wing.

Remove the tape from the assembly, and cut the right wing to the same length as the left. I would recommend using manicure scissors to do this. Next, you should cut the horizontal stabilizers to length.

Trim the fuselage fore and aft. You are now the proud owner of a rudderless N scale model airplane.

To make the models in Z, HO, S, and O multiply the dimensions for N by .75, 2, 2.5, and 3, respectively. You'll probably want to cement a ver-

tical stabilizer (rudder) to the tail for scales larger than HO.

Hold the other end of the tether about ½″ from the end, heat it to cherry red, and insert it in the hand and arm of the miniature figure. The figure is ready to cement to the shaft of a 4- to 6-rpm Hankscraft or Haydon clock motor. For finishing touches treat the tether wire with Hobby Black and paint the plane a bright color.

Record the sound of a model airplane in flight on a continuous loop tape, and you'll have a credible animated display. Here's hoping these two projects will help you "get things moving" on your model railroad.

9

Tale of a Turning Head

By John Armstrong
Photos by the author

At last – an O scale engineer who watches where he's going

A little impatient and raring to go, Casey peers intently back, awaiting a hand signal from his crew as they set out a car.

Son of a gun! Casey has turned his head and is training his eagle eye forward as he heads on up the line on the author's O scale Canandaigua Southern.

Next to the trains themselves, what are the most eye-catching elements in railroading? Usually, people!

And what is the most interesting thing a person does on a railroad? Why, run the locomotive, of course! Sooner or later, then, most of us want to add engineers to our engines. And true to that old hymn about the perils of mountain railroading, once that brave fellow is soldered or glued to his seat box, he faithfully "keeps his hand upon the throttle and his eye upon the rail." Nor does he ever even bat that eye.

The engineer's state of suspended animation is not too much of a strain on reality in the case of a road locomotive, but in switching and local-freight situations the engineer's eagle eye is peering in the wrong direction at least half the time.

After a couple of decades of contemplating an improvement I was lured by the roomy and empty cab interior of Weaver's O scale RS-3 into what promised to be a nice little weekend project.

Design considerations

I thought the engineer ought to look forward when the engine was moving forward and backwards while it was in reverse. When stopped, the best scenario was that he look backwards, as if waiting for a signal from his switch operators.

Accepting rather brain-jarring head-snaps, I decided on a solenoid to turn the head to the forward-peer-

ing attitude at the start of forward motion with spring-return to a quizzical backward look ("What are those clowns arguing about now?") at all other times. All it would take would be a crank to convert the lateral motion of a solenoid's plunger to a realistic degree of neck rotation.

Owls, though stuck with immovable eyeballs, keep watch by swiveling their heads more than 180 degrees. For us, 140 degrees or so should suffice—taking into account eye movement, which—thankfully—is too small to model in any of our scales. Our hogger will probably be facing as much downward as backward when not watching the way ahead. As fig. 1 shows, however, a simple crank won't quite achieve this without running into dead-center problems.

Gears to the rescue

An accumulation of "too good to throw away" plastic gears from electric typewriter cloth-ribbon cartridges provided a neat answer to this problem. See fig. 2. (The once-through carbon-ribbon cartridges generally don't contain such goodies.) The gear ratio is approximately 2:1, and the price is unbeatable.

In such a noncritical application, of course, any reasonably fine-pitch gears will work—even homemade kinds with hand-filed notches vaguely resembling gear teeth. These little fellows are particularly handy though, since the big ones are thick enough to

stay in line without the formality of pivot bearings, and the little one can be bored to fit and attached with epoxy to a spindle fabricated using "the poor man's lathe"—telescoping brass tubing. K&S is the brand you'll usually see in hobby shops.

From here on, the description of my head-turning mechanism hits the high points of only one way (and almost assuredly not the best one) of skinning this cat, based on the parts and techniques I had available, along with the dimensions and characteristics of this particular locomotive kit.

Installation

The space in the cab and under the hood had looked so ample to start. But it shrank drastically when matched against the size of parts that would do the job.

The RS-3 cab readily slides up and off, though if the results of our project are to be conspicuous enough to be worthwhile our engineer's head and shoulder must stick well outside the window. This means finding some way to put at least these parts of him in place after the cab is in place. See fig. 3.

To accommodate Casey to the narrow RS-3 window meant dismembering him into four segments respectively glued to, hanging from, slid onto, and keyed to the cab seat, control stand (an oversize and only impressionistically prototypical fake conjured up mainly to cover the gears) cab window arm rest, and rotating "spinal column."

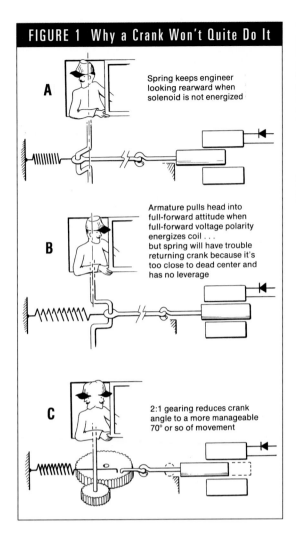

FIGURE 1 Why a Crank Won't Quite Do It

A
Spring keeps engineer looking rearward when solenoid is not energized

B
Armature pulls head into full-forward attitude when full-forward voltage polarity energizes coil . . .
but spring will have trouble returning crank because it's too close to dead center and has no leverage

C
2:1 gearing reduces crank angle to a more manageable 70° or so of movement

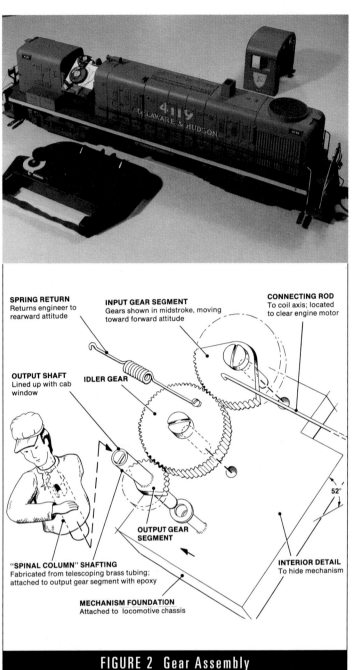

SPRING RETURN
Returns engineer to rearward attitude

INPUT GEAR SEGMENT
Gears shown in midstroke, moving toward forward attitude

CONNECTING ROD
To coil axis; located to clear engine motor

OUTPUT SHAFT
Lined up with cab window

IDLER GEAR

"SPINAL COLUMN" SHAFTING
Fabricated from telescoping brass tubing; attached to output gear segment with epoxy

OUTPUT GEAR SEGMENT

MECHANISM FOUNDATION
Attached to locomotive chassis

INTERIOR DETAIL
To hide mechanism

52°

FIGURE 2 Gear Assembly

Fig. 2. Photo. We can see the gears that turn Casey's head, as well as the Silver-Reed Ex-42 typewriter ribbon cartridge that provided said gears. Unused segments of the input and output gears were cut away. Forward of the middle (or idler) gear is the spring that returns Casey's head to the rearward position. The spring, which is shaped something like a pretzel run amuck, was—in the author's words—"designed with pliers in a strictly trial-and-error procedure." Not visible, under the forward hood, is the solenoid that powers the mechanism.

Consequently it was easier to build him up from scratch than to try to adapt an available metal or plastic figure. I carved Casey from acrylic plastic with a cutter in a motor tool. An essential feature, of course, is his traditional long-billed Kromer railroad cap—we want it obvious which way he's looking.

Electrically speaking, the old and the new

As the wiring schematic of fig. 4 shows, the basic circuit is simply a head-turning solenoid coil that is energized by propulsion power whenever its polarity (as detected by a diode in series) indicates a desire for forward motion. Since the solenoid must overcome not only all friction in the mechanical system but also a spring-return force sufficient to return all parts to zero against that same friction, a fairly good pull over a distance of more than a third of an inch is required. My solution was to adapt the coil and plunger of a well-seasoned Lionel E unit from my "still might be useful someday" stockpile. [E units are the reversing mechanisms in some Lionel locomotives. —Ed.]

Winding a coil like this (approximately ⅝" o.d. x ⅞" long, surrounding an iron armature sliding in a core tube about ¼" in diameter) from scratch would also be no big deal, assuming suitable magnet wire (no. 31 or thereabouts) is at hand.

[Solenoids of various sizes are available at electronics stores, although as far as we know Radio Shack doesn't carry any. Newark Electronics shows in their catalog some Guardian models that should be up to the job. —Ed.]

Depending on motor and drive characteristics, however, a solenoid that has enough resistance to stay cool on full voltage still may not generate enough magnetic pull (which is proportional to amperes multiplied by turns) to rotate Casey's head before the voltage rises to a level that will start the engine moving, particularly on a slight downgrade or without cars. Enter some modern electronics.

It would be almost sinful to put so competent an engineman in a locomotive without direction-responsive, constant-intensity headlights, so the diagram includes today's silicon diodes to accomplish all these purposes. With the dropping diodes regulating the headlight voltage in series with the armature but not the head-turning coil, the resulting net 1.9 voltage differential against motor-start may suffice. If not, the diagram includes optional ballast and compensating resistors (R1 and R2) to tweak up the head-turn/engine motion sequence and—if that is important in your scheme of operation—equalize locomotive performance in forward and reverse directions.

What we end up with here is something akin to a diesel Shay—a locomotive that loses pizazz if not pointed so you can see its right-side-only action. Fortunately, at the expense of extended neck strain on its hogger, our local freight typically works an out-and-back schedule that keeps him on the aisle side both ways.

The project ended up presenting more challenges than even a completely unencumbered weekend could have overcome. Still, the effectiveness of Casey's motion in attracting attention to an otherwise prosaic model has made the project worthwhile, as have reflections on how much tougher it would have been within the confines of a steam switcher cab.

Fig. 3. Top: This photo with the cab removed gives a good sense of how the engineer is installed. The quasi-control stand, painted a hopefully inconspicuous black, hides the gears that turn his head. Above: The engineer was made in four pieces. The thighs and left arm are glued inside the cab. The body and rotating head are separate and slip over the brass tube "spinal column" from outside after the cab is in place. The brass tubing neck is slotted and slips over a keyway rod in the drive shaft.

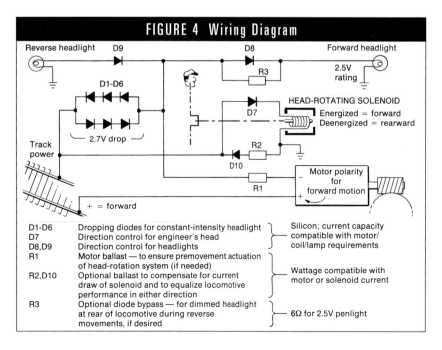

FIGURE 4 Wiring Diagram		
D1-D6	Dropping diodes for constant-intensity headlight	Silicon; current capacity compatible with motor/ coil/lamp requirements
D7	Direction control for engineer's head	
D8,D9	Direction control for headlights	
R1	Motor ballast — to ensure premovement actuation of head-rotation system (if needed)	Wattage compatible with motor or solenoid current
R2,D10	Optional ballast to compensate for current draw of solenoid and to equalize locomotive performance in either direction	
R3	Optional diode bypass — for dimmed headlight at rear of locomotive during reverse movements, if desired	6Ω for 2.5V penlight

10

Magic Water

By Lee Vande Visse
Photos by the author

USE A TWO-WAY MIRROR AND SOME TINSEL
TO SIMULATE MOVING WATER

Creating the illusion of movement is the most difficult aspect of modeling water, but it's not impossible. I call my technique "Magic water" after the name given it by one of the younger operators on my On3 Crown Mountain RR.

Two-way mirror

The heart of this project is a two-way mirror, one that reflects like a normal mirror as long as the area behind it is dark. Once you place a light behind the mirror, the light overwhelms the normal surface reflectivity and the light and objects around it become visible as the intensity is increased.

A number of mirror sizes are available from American Science Center (601 Linden Place, Evanston, IL 60202) and Edmund Scientific (101 East Gloucester Pike, Barrington, NJ 08007).

I began by locating the lake and future bridge after the plywood sub-roadbed was in place, but before any scenery was built. I used an 8″ x 10″ mirror which I mounted about 5″ below the future track level. This allowed plenty of room for the bridge and created a large enough lake so my efforts were clearly visible.

Some two-way mirrors have a

silver coating on one side, which should be installed down.

I supported the mirror using four small pieces of scrap 1 x 2 lumber, one under each corner, as shown in fig. 1. It's important to mount the mirror level. A hot glue gun makes it easy to fabricate the supporting framework, which should prevent the mirror from flexing or cracking.

The blocks supporting the mirror shouldn't extend more than an inch under the edges or they'll become visible. Paint these blocks flat black.

Once the mirror is in place, finish the surrounding scenery, making sure the plaster forms a tight seal all the way around the mirror's surface. When you're done with the scenery, there should be no bare white plaster showing along the edge between the plaster and the glass.

Scrape any dried paint and plaster blobs from the mirror with a razor blade and polish the surface clean.

Mixing water

For the water surface I used polyester casting resin distributed by the ETI Company (P. O. Box 95537, Fields Landing, CA 95537). Other brands are available at craft and hobby shops. The big problem with this material is that as it cures it gives off noxious fumes. Read the label: It gives a complete warning about this.

Another familiar material, Enviro-Tex, doesn't have an odor problem. However, I've found it tends to discolor over time, and I've had problems with trapped air bubbles in cured castings.

Fortunately, my layout room can be isolated from the rest of the house and actively vented to the outside for extended periods, It's a good idea to wear a face mask with two-stage filtration (a respirator) while you're working with resin.

For my 7" x 8" area I used 2 ounces of resin. Don't mix the casting resin in anything you hope to save later—I use paper cups.

As a rule of thumb I use 15 drops of hardener per ounce of resin. I spend at least 5 minutes stirring the mix, as failure to adequately combine the two can mean disaster in the form of a lake that never dries.

As I was stirring, I added three drops of blue food coloring per ounce of resin. You can experiment with color variations in small batches.

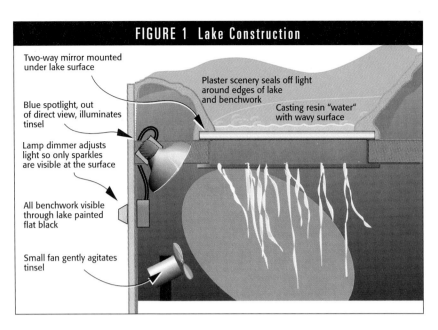

FIGURE 1 Lake Construction

Two-way mirror mounted under lake surface

Plaster scenery seals off light around edges of lake and benchwork

Blue spotlight, out of direct view, illuminates tinsel

Casting resin "water" with wavy surface

Lamp dimmer adjusts light so only sparkles are visible at the surface

All benchwork visible through lake painted flat black

Small fan gently agitates tinsel

Since a light will eventually be placed below the mirror and shine through the casting resin, the color should be a bit darker than for normal viewing.

Making waves

Pour the mixture on the mirror and spread it around with the help of a small "T" made from two pieces of stripwood glued together. Use it like a broom to push the mixture evenly around the surface.

You'll have about a half hour of working time. Check the resin by periodically touching it with a piece of stripwood. The drying time varies with several factors, including brand and temperature, so it's best not to always trust the clock.

When the mixture began to thicken, I added 15 more drops of hardener across the surface. Then, using the same piece of test stripwood, I drew parallel furrows in the resin. These waves should slowly settle back to flat after a few seconds. I repeated this procedure every 10 or 15 seconds.

Finally the waves don't settle back down—they stay in place. At this point the casting resin has solidified, and with it the waves.

I gave it a good look, then closed the door to the layout room for two or three days because this stuff really stinks. If possible leave a window open with a fan running to vent the area.

Making the water move

If this were all there were to the project the lake would still look pretty good, but here's where the fun begins.

I placed a 60-watt colored spotlight a foot or so below the underside of the lake bottom, mounting it on an adjustable stand as shown in fig. 1. It should be plugged into an outlet or extension cord with a dimmer switch.

I prefer a blue light but you can experiment with color. The beam must illuminate the lake, but the spotlight should be out of sight from above.

By adjusting the intensity and position of the light you can reach a balance that gives the lake a dramatic appearance. If you see any of the surrounding benchwork through the lake, paint it flat black and it will disappear. One of the advantages of the casting resin waves is that they knock the view of the underside out of focus.

Once again, if we stopped here the project would be good enough, but this is where we add motion.

As shown in fig. 1, suspend Christmas tinsel below the surface of the mirror. Be generous in your use of the tinsel and spray the upper portions of these hangers with cheap flat black spray paint. This hides the exposed stripwood and upper portions of tinsel.

The last step is to install a small, quiet fan, which gently sways the tinsel in the spotlight. I built the fan using spare parts and an old 12-volt motor. I used a plug-in transformer for power, one of those little black plastic boxes that plug into the wall.

By experimenting and adjusting the speed of the fan and the intensity of the spotlight, you can create various effects and produce a surprisingly—almost magically—realistic lake.

11

Video Animation

By D. Derek Verner
Photos by the author

ADD LIFE TO YOUR LAYOUT WITH A VCR AND MINI-TV

There's a party going on in this HO model building, thanks to Derek Verner's video animation techniques.

Most of the time our trains rumble through towns and countryside that are bereft of animation. In fact, when we hear that word we often think of mechanical devices, such as crossing gates, that are herky-jerky and toy-like, but here's a way to add action to a layout with a miniature TV set. Consider the following:

"Can't they go any faster?" asks your nonrailroading visitor. Suddenly from the corner of his eye, he catches a flash of movement in one of the illuminated foreground buildings. He steps closer and peers in the window. Inside, people less than an inch high are having a party. Couples are dancing and two guys with electric guitars are wailing away. He can hear heavy metal music apparently blaring from their tiny amplifiers.

A light goes on in the apartment next door and a middle-aged couple in bathrobes pound on the adjoining wall. Then the husband strides to his door and steps out. Shortly after, the party's host opens his door in response to insistent knocking. An argument ensues.

The visitor turns from the scene in disbelief. "Are those kids having another party?" you casually inquire. The party-goers are video images you've reproduced on a mini-TV set concealed within the structure. A VCR feeds the signal from a tape starring your friends and family.

What you'll need

You can use the family VCR to feed signals to the TV, and you don't even need to locate it in your train room.

The next item is a video camera or camcorder. You only need the camera during production and can borrow or rent it. The last major item is a mini-TV. These are available in black and white or color, with screen diagonals of 1.6″ to 5″. Prices start around $60, and you can install the set so it can be easily removed to watch the ball game.

Most of the mini color sets are LCD (liquid crystal display) types and are highly directional. If you look at them off-axis, strange things happen to brightness and contrast. For this reason, special precautions must be taken to control the angle of viewing which are described later in the mini-TV installation section.

A better image is produced by a CRT (cathode ray tube) display like those used on standard TV sets.

Unfortunately, I haven't been able to find a CRT color set with a screen smaller than 5″. Surprisingly though, black and white is very effective.

Getting started

Step 1 is hooking up the camera to the mini-TV. Follow the instructions that come with the camera.

Once you're getting the image on the TV from the camera, prepare a diagram like the one in fig. 1. If your video camera is equipped with a zoom lens, set it to its widest angle. Point the camera at a distant object that fills the screen from side to side, then measure the distance from the object to the camera lens.

Next, measure the width of the object. Use these two measurements to construct triangle A-B-C in the scale you model. This represents the widest angle of view to which your camera can be set. Next measure the width of your screen in your modeling scale and transfer this measurement to the diagram, shown as line D-E. Now, measure line B-F in scale feet. This distance (in real feet) is how far your camera must be from the subject to produce an image on the screen that is in proper scale.

For most cameras this distance is longer than most rooms, an obvious difficulty when it comes to producing your tape. There are solutions:

You can add an auxiliary wide-angle adapter lens available from video suppliers, or you can shoot in a theater, gymnasium, or outdoors using the side of a building as a backdrop.

The final suggestion, which will be discussed next, is to use the camcorder to tape partial frame images from a regular TV playing the original tape. Because our final image is so small, the decrease in quality will not be noticeable.

Multiple images

To create the party scene described earlier you'll want activity in two rooms, so you'll need to divide the screen into different areas. Figure 2 shows how I did this for four areas.

Figure 3 shows a matte box attached to the front of a video camera. With such a box you can block out portions of the image during taping. On mine a sliding panel and a piece of black cardboard can be adjusted to mask out the portions of the screen that are to remain dark. You can jury-rig something out of cardboard. Be sure the inside is black and the mattes are far enough away from the lens to produce a sharp edge when the camera is focused on the subject.

Since our goal is to produce four areas where animated images can appear, we don't need to tape our original footage from such a great distance after all, as we'll be reshooting off the TV screen. Since each scene represents a fourth of the mini-TV's screen area, it can be shot from half the distance.

If you choose this method, the original tapes should be shot without the matte box so they fill the viewfinder. When you reshoot them from the large TV screen onto the four different areas, you can do it in a darkened room, and again the matte box won't be needed.

Mini-TV installation

Now decide what sort of model building will house the TV set. Will it be an office, factory, or apartment? It must be large enough to house the mini-TV with the screen set back from the windows.

Design a method to hold the TV in position yet allow it to be removed easily. The box and room shown in figs. 4 and 5 are examples of ways to help control the angle of viewing. You can provide access from beneath the layout or make the building so it can be lifted off its foundation. Provide paths for the power cable (usually a wall transformer) and the signal cable.

If smart domestic relations require your VCR to be in another room, you

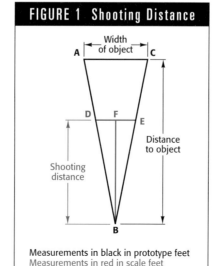

FIGURE 1 Shooting Distance

Width of object

A C

D F E

Distance to object

Shooting distance

B

Measurements in black in prototype feet
Measurements in red in scale feet

Fig. 2 MULTIPLE SCENES. The screen can be divided using a grease pencil to allow animation in several different areas.

can run cable or use a wireless transmitter called "The Rabbit" which is available for under $30. It can transmit the audio and video signals from the VCR at distances up to 120 feet, enabling you to watch tapes being played on a single VCR from receiver-equipped television sets located in other parts of the house. Extra receivers cost about $15 each.

The television image shown in fig. 6 is from a black-and-white CRT, and while I was pleased with the clarity of the images, I didn't care for the "color"—it appeared too blue. For this reason, and to provide variety in the lighting of the four areas, I used different theatrical gels (which are available at theatrical supply stores) on the windows of each apartment. Browns and ambers worked well and warmed up the scenes to make the lighting appear incandescent.

Shooting the production

The animation scenario you decide to shoot should be short—no longer than a minute or two—and it should contain as much action and

Fig. 3 MATTE BOX. A box fitted to the front of the camera (left) permits shooting images confined to particular areas on the tape.

Fig. 4 TV BOX. Derek built an .080″ styrene box to fit snugly over and hold this mini-TV set. The box was then mounted inside an HO scale building.

Fig. 5 CONTROLLING THE VIEW. A "room" added to the front of the box controls the angle at which the screen can be viewed.

Fig. 6 FINAL INSTALLATION. Left: A wood block holds the TV set in its frame. Since even small **LCD** television sets generate some heat, it's best to leave the glazing out of most windows to allow the heat to escape. Theatrical gel samples can be used to change the apparent color of the illumination in the room. Above: A black-and-white **TV** image without gels has a blue tinge.

movement as possible. Show the kids playing with the dog, someone vacuum cleaning, or a forklift being driven around a warehouse. It's the movement that will attract the visitor to the window.

Set the camera on a tripod or other stable support at about eye level. Tape speed should be standard, or SP, because our final tape will be second generation and we want to preserve as much image quality as possible.

If your camera is far from the action, you can place a microphone in the scene to pick up the sounds. Also some VCRs allow you to add sound later.

The idea is to shoot one or more short sequences and then loop them to create a final two-hour tape with random intervals of action. It's the lights going on and off and flashes of movement that catch your eye. You can have one of your actors flip a wall switch at the beginning and end

of each sequence to justify the effect.

Keep props and sets as simple as possible. This is particularly true if you include three-dimensional objects in the room as shown in fig. 5. If it doesn't move or get moved, leave it out. This also simplifies shooting if you are forced outdoors to use the side of a building as a backdrop.

Making the final tape

Since the final production tape will run for two hours with the action taking place at intervals, it's essential that the screen go dark between these intervals. Blank tape played on a VCR produces a raster pattern. Therefore, the final tape must be prerecorded with "video black." To prepare your final tape, leave the audio cables disconnected, rewind the tape, place the lens cap on the camera, press RECORD on the VCR and let it run to the end.

Reconnect the audio cables,

rewind the tape, and locate the first sequence you want to copy onto the final tape. Press PLAY on the camcorder and RECORD on the VCR to copy the sequence. When it's over, stop the VCR and camcorder and find the second sequence or rewind the camcorder to the beginning of the same sequence. Press PLAY or FAST FORWARD on the VCR for an interval of black. Repeat until the tape is filled.

All that remains is to connect the VCR to your TV and play your masterwork. Keep the volume at a low level; it should only be audible once your visitor's attention has been drawn to the scene.

Video and film making can be confusing at first, but both are fascinating. The late, great Orson Welles was once asked how he liked making films. Reaching for the ultimate complimentary metaphor, he replied, "It's the greatest train set a boy can have."

12

Brighten Up Your World

By Gregory H. Heier

LIGHTING FOR REALISM

Creating a dramatic night scene like this one on Al Kubicka's HO scale Panhandle Route takes a variety of individual light sources following stage lighting techniques. Greg Heier photo

Good lighting is one of the last frontiers model railroaders are discovering in their ongoing quest for realism. It's essential for displaying good modeling, while poor lighting only highlights flaws. The importance of lighting is vividly demonstrated on Al Kubicka's HO scale Panhandle Route.

Room preparations

The Panhandle Route is located in a windowless room with track lights on the 15-foot-high ceiling. This lighting has its own dimmers, making it possible to shift from white daylight lamps to blue moonlight, or to a night sky filled with thunder and lightning.

Backdrops were installed and painted before the layout was built, including a mountain scene on the west wall painted by a professional artist. The mountains are backed by eight feet of plain sky which reflects simulated lightning from a projector in the ceiling.

Al painted the rural backdrop and clouds on the other walls so they blend with the modeled foreground features.

He also created a cityscape using several Walthers backgrounds and a three-dimensional overlapping technique. He glued the printed scenes onto tempered hardboard, carefully cut them out, and layered the cutouts along the wall. Al used various thicknesses of foam spacers to create separation and add to the apparent depth of the scene.

To further enhance the depth, five-volt lamps are strung behind the first level. This adds contrast as well as a bright glow to the rear layer of flats creating the ambiance of the city.

Power for the miniature lamps, switch motors, and structure interior lamps is provided by power supplies salvaged from obsolete computers.

Street and building lights

The streetlights are Model Power items suitable for Al's mid-1950s era. They come with 16-volt lamps that look slightly yellow when powered by a 12-volt supply, but the lower voltage greatly extends their life-span.

Canopy and building eave lights are 14-volt grain-of-rice lamps. For interior lighting, larger pilot lamps do the job. They're low-voltage lamps commonly used in the days before small LEDs (light-emitting diodes). Al was able to locate and purchase several hundred in a surplus shop for only $5.

Bare-lead lamps

The biggest secret of realistic lighting is the use of a lot of bare-lead miniature lamps. Al uses many 14V, 40 milliamp bare-lead subminiature lamps in his structures. These bulbs are of uniform size and have 3″ tinned leads for easy soldering.

Above: Interior lighting and big windows often make it necessary to complete interior details which become visible once the lights are on. This is an O scale drug store that Al built. Greg Heier photo

Above left: Overall room lighting is provided with white and blue floodlights connected to separate dimmer-controlled circuits. They're easily adjusted for different times of the day. Harold Krewer photo

Left: With a little planning, tiny lamps may be added under station roof eaves to illuminate the walking areas which are normally lighted for safety and convenience. Harold Krewer photo

Many realistic lighting effects use these tiny lamps including:

• Porch lights made by using a single lamp hung under a porch roof. Brass wire downspouts carry the power.

• Station canopy lights hung from a pair of brass rods running the length of the roof. At the ends of the canopy, the feeder wires are bent like drain pipes.

• Gooseneck lamps added to a coaling tower by coating the bare leads with clear nail polish for insulation, shaping them into a gooseneck, and mounting the lamp in a hole drilled into the wall.

• Eave lights along the roof edges and over the agent's desk inside.

The trick here is to be observant and try to re-create effects you see.

Lamp life and access

Lamps are most affected by voltage. By using 10 to 12 volts instead of the rated 14 volts, lamp life may be extended by several decades.

Lamps also last longer when used on AC instead of DC. Lamp life is affected by the number of on and off cycles, as well as the size of the initial voltage spike when they're first turned on.

As lamps are added, Heier's corollary to Murphy's Model Railroad Law comes into play: "The more inaccessible a lamp, or the more difficult a lamp is to replace, the shorter its lifespan will be."

Creating realism

If you want your lighting to look realistic, you need to think like a stage lighting director, analyzing the direction and intensity of every light:

• Study the world around you, taking notice of how light plays on everyday objects. Notice how the atmosphere dims and reddens lights in the distance.

• Highlight the details by putting light in the areas that you want people to notice. Light draws the eye,

so you can direct your visitors' attention to your best finished scenes.

• Keep light levels low. From a hilltop even the brightest lights look subdued and the coverage of any particular lamp is limited. Too much light makes a scene look artificial, and bright interior lights make buildings look toylike.

• Use backlighting to outline building silhouettes and add depth with lights between and behind the building flats.

• Blend the lighting so overhead blue moonlight doesn't overwhelm the structure lights. A moonless night is truly black—except for ambient light created by humans.

• Detail structure interiors if guests can get close enough to notice these items. Big windows and interior lights make this time and effort worthwhile.

On with the show

Hobby pioneer Frank Ellison often compared model railroad operations with stage plays, and there's nowhere in the hobby where this is more apparent than in lighting. Don't be afraid to experiment and move things around. A small shift in shadows can do wonders.

If you're not careful, you may find it's more enjoyable to run your railroad during the night shift!

13

Diode Lighting Made Easy

By Bill De Foe
Photos by the author

FUN FOR THOSE WHO DON'T UNDERSTAND ELECTRONICS

Lots of modelers are afraid of electronics. The minute words like "transistor" or "diode" are mentioned they turn the page. If you're one of these people, then this article is especially for you. I'll show you how easy it is to install diode lighting.

Constant intensity headlight

Let's start with a constant intensity locomotive headlight. You need only one electronic component, a Radio Shack no. 276-1152 bridge rectifier costing around $1.19. Add to this a Pacific Fast Mail no. PFM-13 1.5-volt micro-miniature bulb and an MV

Products headlight lens, and you have the complete project.

Take a look at the bridge rectifier shown in fig. 1. There are four wire leads, one of which is marked with either a plus sign or a dot. This is the positive lead. The one directly opposite it is the negative lead, and the other two are called the AC leads. Our first step is to twist the positive and negative leads tightly together, cut off the excess wire, and solder them.

A few words of caution about soldering the bridge rectifier: It's a solid-state device and can be damaged by too much heat. Do not use a sol-

Diode lighting adds excitement and realism to the author's HO locomotive fleet. Besides a constant intensity headlight, this engine is equipped with class lights and a fire glowing in the firebox.

dering gun. Use a low-wattage pencil-type iron rated between 30 and 45 watts and allow the iron to heat up fully before attempting the job.

Soldering with an iron that hasn't reached sufficient heat transmits more heat into the device than soldering quickly with a hot iron. As with any electronic circuit, use a good 60:40 rosin-core solder; never use an acid-type flux. If you don't own a pencil-type soldering iron, you can get one from Radio Shack for about the price of a good boxcar kit.

Next remove one wire from the locomotive motor (it doesn't matter which one), and insert the bridge rectifier, running the motor current through the two remaining AC leads. Now was that so hard? Except for the bulb itself, your circuit is finished.

Before adding the bulb test-run the locomotive in both directions. This is very important! If the rectifier was damaged by too much heat or is defective, an installed bulb will go off like a flashbulb.

If your locomotive won't run or runs in only one direction, either the rectifier is bad and must be replaced or you didn't solder the leads properly.

Headlight installation

I install my bulbs in MV Products headlight lenses, first grinding a tiny pocket in the center of the silvered side, using the smallest Dremel ball-tip cutter available (fig. 2). Once I attach the tip of the bulb with epoxy, it looks like a bulb in the center of a reflector!

After fitting the bulb/reflector assembly into the headlight casing, I secure it with a spot of super glue from the rear to avoid marring the front lens surface. Then I tack-solder the two wires from the PFM bulb to the bridge rectifier's AC leads to complete the circuit.

That's all there is to it! When reassembling the locomotive I'm very careful that the bare wires on the bridge rectifier don't touch any metal inside the engine. Just one note of caution: steer clear of old or cheaply made motors. If they pull too much current, they'll burn out the bridge rectifier and POP! go the PFM bulbs.

You should realize that we aren't using the bridge rectifier for its intended purpose. If you tell a computer or TV repairman that you're soldering the plus and minus leads together and running DC through the AC inputs, he will look at you as though you were crazy and say, "It'll never work." Just snicker to yourself.

Locomotive classification lights

Utah Pacific makes HO scale hollow brass marker light castings (item no. 63) that can be drilled out with a ¹⁄₁₆″ drill to accept the PFM microbulbs. Securing the bulbs into the castings with epoxy while illuminating them with a 1.5-volt flashlight battery allows you to align the brightest part of the bulb filament with the openings in the casting (fig. 3). I use Radio Shack five-minute epoxy for this because it sets fast and dries clear.

For colored lenses I must give credit to Adolph Frank. He suggested sealing the marker openings with a tiny drop of Elmer's white glue (it usually takes at least two applications, as the glue shrinks). When the glue has dried, I color the lenses with fine-point felt-tip markers. Thank you, Adolph!

If your locomotive class lights are white, they will probably be too bright, making your locomotive look as if it has three headlights. To dim them connect one wire from each class light bulb and solder them to a 5-ohm, ¼-watt resistor. Radio Shack no longer sells a 5-ohm resistor in this size; if you can't find one elsewhere, two Radio Shack no. 271-1301 10-ohm resistors can be placed side by side and will give you the equivalent of 5 ohms resistance. See fig. 3.

Here's a way to solve a problem and gain a fire in your firebox at the same time. The problem comes when we use diode lighting with the newer can motors. I like my engines to sit motionless with lights lit by maintaining a low voltage on the track at all times. This works great with the older open-frame motors, but the newer can types draw so little current and start turning at such a low voltage that the engine is moving before the lights come on.

Figure 4 shows how this problem can be minimized and sometimes eliminated by wiring a 12-volt grain-of-wheat bulb directly across the motor terminals. Not only does this bulb add resistance, but you can dye it orange or red and place it between the locomotive frame sides and below the firebox for use as a firebox glow.

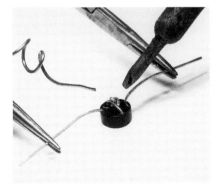

FIG. 1. INSTALLING BRIDGE RECTIFIERS
Top left: Here's a bridge rectifier right out of the package. Top right: The author modifies it by connecting the positive and negative leads and soldering them. Above: The device is cut into one side of the motor circuit. After testing, the headlight bulb will be added.

Fig. 2. HEADLIGHT. After drilling a hole in an MV Products lens, the author uses epoxy to attach the bulb.

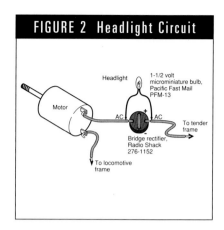

FIGURE 2 Headlight Circuit

Universal 1.5-volt power supply

Since I use a lot of PFM 1.5-volt micro-miniature bulbs, I designed a universal 1.5-volt power supply for them. It works for constant intensity lighting in my cabooses, passenger cars, structures, and streetlights. With a slight modification it can be used for directional backup lights on my locomotive tenders.

The universal power supply is almost as simple as the locomotive headlight circuit and can be built for about $2. It consists of two components: a no. 194 automobile bulb, available at gas stations, and a Radio Shack no. 276-1152 bridge rectifier. Again, you solder the plus and minus leads of the rectifier together and cut them short.

Now solder one of the bridge rectifier's AC leads to one of the auto bulb leads. These leads usually seem to have a coating of oil, so clean them first in dishwashing detergent so the solder will flow better.

The input voltage is applied to the remaining auto bulb lead and the remaining rectifier lead. The 1.5-volt output is tapped off on each side of the rectifier on the AC leads as you did before (fig. 5).

The power supply will accept any input from 3 to 12 volts, and either AC or DC. For the lights in my rolling stock I use track power. The lights will come on as the track power reaches about 3 volts, and then will maintain a constant intensity over the remainder of the speed (voltage) range.

For cabooses and passenger cars, I run one input lead to each truck. Of course, the uninsulated wheels must be on opposite sides of the car, and at least one truck must be insulated from the frame. You can paint the automobile bulb black to eliminate the glow and hide it and the bridge rectifier inside a washroom or tool locker if interior detail is added.

Power supplies to be used under the layout I mount on small wood blocks and add terminal strips to make wiring easier. I mount these supplies with a single wood screw.

Power for my under-the-layout

supplies comes from a 6.3-volt filament transformer taken from an old tube-type radio and mounted behind the control panel. Wires from this are run to the universal power supplies.

It's important that the power supplies be near the devices they power. Voltage will drop with long runs of wire, and when you're starting with only 1.5 volts it doesn't take much drop to affect the brightness of the bulbs. So keep the 1.5-volt wires short. It doesn't matter if the 6.3-volt AC line drops because the power supplies will work at half that value.

In theory, you could use a 12.6-volt transformer instead of the 6.3-volt one, but I don't recommend it due to the excessive heat buildup that could occur.

Caution! One side of these filament transformers must be wired to 115 volts. This can be dangerous! If you don't know how to do this safely, have an electrician help.

A good alternative to the 6.3-volt transformer would be a dedicated HO power pack with the throttle set to deliver around 6 volts. Don't use a cheap one, though, if you plan to

FIG. 3. CLASS LIGHTS. The author uses a battery to test-power a microbulb while positioning it for the best effect when installed in a marker light.

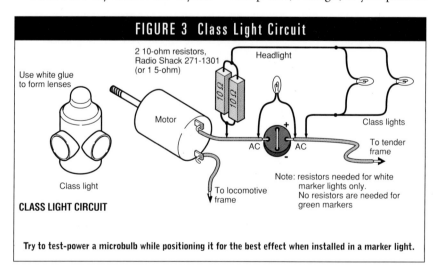

FIGURE 3 Class Light Circuit

Try to test-power a microbulb while positioning it for the best effect when installed in a marker light.

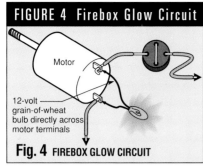

FIGURE 4 Firebox Glow Circuit

Motor

12-volt grain-of-wheat bulb directly across motor terminals

Fig. 4 FIREBOX GLOW CIRCUIT

FIG. 5. UNIVERSAL 1.5-VOLT POWER SUPPLY
Above: This under-the-table model includes terminal strips for easy wiring. It can be mounted to the layout with a wood screw. Below: This version of the same power supply is cemented to the floor of a tender.

Output 1.5 volts

No.194 automobile bulb

AC   AC

Bridge rectifier, Radio Shack 276-1152

Input 3-12 volts AC or DC

UNIVERSAL POWER SUPPLY

CINDER VALLEY

power several of the these power supplies or build one of the heavy-duty supplies I'll describe shortly. You need enough power to handle your total load.

These small power supplies are limited to powering three PFM bulbs. For four or more bulbs in a single location, you'll need a heavier power supply. Making one is easy, as shown in fig. 6. Just replace the no. 194 auto-mobile bulb with a taillight/stoplight bulb and the small bridge rectifier with a 4-amp Radio Shack no. 276-1146 unit. All wiring remains exactly the same as before. This heavy-duty supply will light a dozen PFM bulbs.

Tender backup light

There are two ways to wire a tender backup light, each with certain advantages and disadvantages. We can either treat the locomotive and tender as two separate pieces of rolling stock with individual lighting circuits or consider them a single unit. See fig. 7.

The first method (fig. 7a) treats the tender as a separate piece of rolling stock and uses the universal power supply circuit and another diode (Radio Shack no. 276-1101) as a switch to turn the circuit on and off. The three components may be wired in any order, but if the light comes on when the engine moves forward, turn the diode around.

The disadvantage to this circuit is that one wire must go from the tender to the locomotive frame. You cannot use the drawbar for this connection because it goes to the motor. You must run a separate wire.

I use this circuit on my Cinder Valley and run two extra wires between the locomotive and tender, disguising them as water hoses. One is used for the backup light circuit, the other as another electrical path for the motor current. If the electrical drawbar loses contact momentarily, the engine won't stutter or stall.

The second circuit shown in fig. 7 treats the locomotive and tender as one unit and doesn't require the additional wire for the backup light. But it does require that you insulate the drawbar pin from the tender frame. It eliminates the no. 194 automobile bulb from the tender and uses the motor in the locomotive as the load for all the lights. A second diode is required in the tender, or else your engine will run only in reverse.

Before you decide which circuit to use, we must discuss how locomotive performance is affected. All locomotives equipped with diode lighting will run slightly slower. This is because each diode in the motor circuit drops the potential top voltage by .75 volt. Within each bridge rectifier we are using two diodes at any given time, so a bridge rectifier in our motor circuit will drop 1.5 volts (the

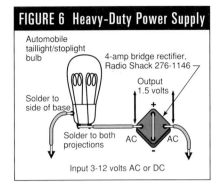

FIGURE 6 Heavy-Duty Power Supply

Automobile taillight/stoplight bulb

4-amp bridge rectifier, Radio Shack 276-1146

Solder to side of base

Output 1.5 volts

Solder to both projections

AC   AC

Input 3-12 volts AC or DC

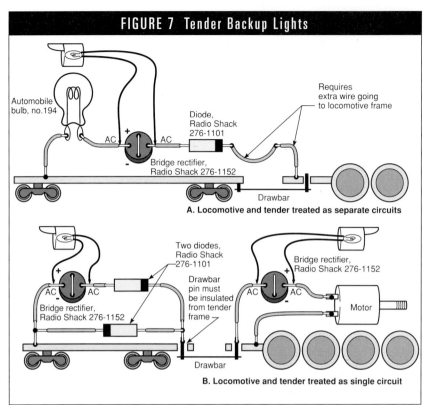

FIGURE 7 Tender Backup Lights

Automobile bulb, no.194

AC + AC

Bridge rectifier, Radio Shack 276-1152

Diode, Radio Shack 276-1101

Requires extra wire going to locomotive frame

Drawbar

A. Locomotive and tender treated as separate circuits

AC   AC

Bridge rectifier, Radio Shack 276-1152

Two diodes, Radio Shack 276-1101

Drawbar pin must be insulated from tender frame

Bridge rectifier, Radio Shack 276-1152

AC   AC

Motor

Drawbar

B. Locomotive and tender treated as single circuit

same 1.5 volts that lights our lamps). This leaves 10.5 volts for the motor when 12 volts are applied to the track. Most of us never run our locomotives at top speed, so the drop doesn't seem too significant.

The circuit in fig. 7b has an additional diode in the forward direction, which drops our top motor power to 9.75 volts, still within our normal operating range.

But take a look at what happens when we run backwards. To light that backup light we must pass the motor current through five diodes, leaving only 8.25 volts for the motor. Fortunately, this happens in only the reverse direction, so if you use the fig. 7b circuit don't expect your locomotive to be a speed demon in reverse.

If you use this second circuit and your backup light comes on in the wrong direction, the easiest way to correct it is to turn the entire tender circuit around with the opposite wire going to the tender frame.

Diesel directional lighting

For diesel directional lighting you need two bridge rectifiers and two diodes. Figure 8 shows how the basic circuit components are electrically oriented, but usually we don't have enough space to lay them out this way.

My Cinder Valley owns only one diesel, an Alco RS-1 by Atlas. Figure 9 shows how I wired it for directional headlights while keeping all the number boards illuminated in both directions. The circuit should work for almost any Atlas/Kato unit.

If I were to do it again, I think I would retain the original 12-volt bulb for the number boards, as the microminiature bulbs don't pass enough light through the long plastic light tubes. This would mean that the number boards would dim at lower speeds, but as it is now they're dim all the time.

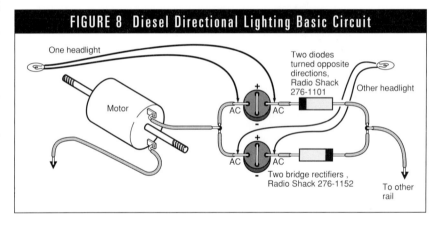

FIGURE 8 Diesel Directional Lighting Basic Circuit

One headlight

Two diodes turned opposite directions, Radio Shack 276-1101

Other headlight

Motor

AC   AC

AC   AC

Two bridge rectifiers, Radio Shack 276-1152

To other rail

First, I freed the short motor tab from underneath the copper wire contact running the length of the engine. After folding the tab back I soldered the banded end of one diode to it, along with a length of insulated wire so I could reach the nonbanded end of the other diode (at the other end of the locomotive).

I attached the bridge rectifiers to the frame with super glue and soldered the free ends of the diodes to one of the AC leads on each bridge. The other AC lead of each bridge was soldered to the original copper contact wire from which I had removed the motor tab. I had to be careful with my soldering so as not to melt any plastic components. Bulb wires were tack-soldered on each side of

the bridges on the AC leads as before.

I cut the original headlight lenses off the light tubes as well as the protrusion that dropped down from each tube and would interfere with the new components. Using super glue I secured a short length of brass tubing into each headlight opening to create a seat for the MV Products lens.

Although I haven't wired an Athearn unit, fig. 10 shows how I would recommend that you do it.

Remove the long metal contact strip that runs the length of the engine. With the locomotive oriented so the metal tabs rising from the trucks are on the side away from you, remove the copper strip, being careful not to lose the motor brush spring. Solder the banded end of one

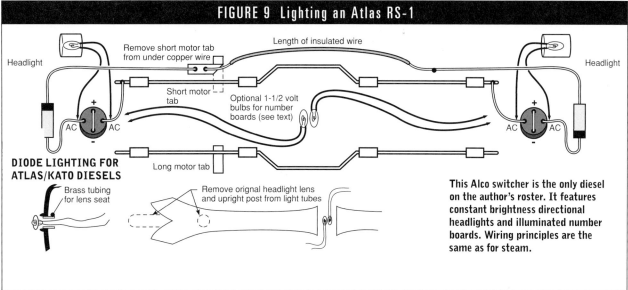

FIGURE 9 Lighting an Atlas RS-1

Headlight

Remove short motor tab from under copper wire

Length of insulated wire

Headlight

Short motor tab

Optional 1-1/2 volt bulbs for number boards (see text)

AC + AC
−

AC + AC
−

DIODE LIGHTING FOR ATLAS/KATO DIESELS

Brass tubing for lens seat

Long motor tab

Remove orignal headlight lens and upright post from light tubes

This Alco switcher is the only diesel on the author's roster. It features constant brightness directional headlights and illuminated number boards. Wiring principles are the same as for steam.

diode to the left end of the copper strip and the nonbanded end to the right end. Replace the copper strip, and cover it completely with electrical insulating tape.

Now snap the long metal contact strip back on and use super glue to attach the bridge rectifiers onto the contact strip next to the first step from the center. One AC lead gets soldered to the contact strip; the other is soldered to the free end of each diode.

Form the wires so the components will reside in the area above the contact strip and below the body shell. Just be sure as you bend them into final position that no diode or bridge rectifier lead touches any metal except that to which it's soldered. Discard the

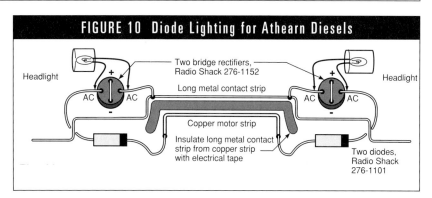

FIGURE 10 Diode Lighting for Athearn Diesels

Headlight

Two bridge rectifiers, Radio Shack 276-1152

Long metal contact strip

Copper motor strip

Insulate long metal contact strip from copper strip with electrical tape

AC + AC
−

AC + AC
−

Headlight

Two diodes, Radio Shack 276-1101

original headlight bulb and bracket.

I hope I've shown how fun and easy diode lighting can be. Believe me, your lighted engines will look great, whether sitting still or on the move. And not only will they be more attractive, they'll be more realistic too.

14

Fiber Optics in Model Railroading

By Lee Vande Visse

CHRISTMAS TREE LIGHTS ARE AN
INEXPENSIVE SOURCE FOR SPECIAL EFFECTS

The author built this shadow box scene to experiment
with fiber optics. Impressive as the photo is, we can't
do the effects justice. The show is spectacular. The
marquee lights chase one another, and those on the cola
sign build in a sequence reminiscent of billboards on
Times Square.

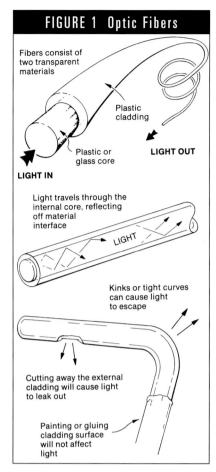

FIGURE 1 Optic Fibers

Fibers consist of two transparent materials

Plastic cladding

Plastic or glass core

LIGHT OUT

LIGHT IN

Light travels through the internal core, reflecting off material interface

LIGHT

Kinks or tight curves can cause light to escape

Cutting away the external cladding will cause light to leak out

Painting or gluing cladding surface will not affect light

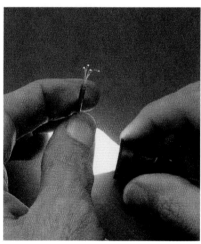

For several years I've been exploring ways to apply fiber optics to the art of model railroading. That's why I built the city scene used to illustrate this article. Here I want to tell you how I used fiber optics in it.

But first some background: Fiber optics have been around since the 1950s. They look like monofilament nylon fishing line, but internally the similarity quickly ends. As shown in fig. 1, these fibers are actually made in two parts, a glass core and the plastic sheath surrounding it.

Light shining into one end passes through the core and out the other end, following any bends in the fiber. A marble, rolling down a hallway and glancing off the walls, is a loose analogy. Both the core and the cladding must be of the highest optical clarity for this to work, and the terms "glass" and "plastic" are over-simplifications for the exotic materials actually used.

The crucial factor is that the interface between the two materials must act to constantly reflect light back into the core and prevent its escape or absorption. This technology has been developed to the point that light loss is now less than 10 percent per kilometer in controlled applications. The benefit to the hobby is that we now have "light tubes" which have an infinite life, are reasonably durable, and can be used almost without regard to length limitations.

Two factors, however, can decrease the effectiveness of the fibers. Despite their appearance they cannot be handled like fishing line. A kink can crush the glass core, and the light will disperse at the point of damage. Before using any strand, test it for bright spots by placing a light bulb at one end. Bright spots along the fiber can indicate damage and should be eliminated.

Also, the more a fiber loops and turns, the more light it will lose. A gradual turn or two will not noticeably affect the output but several tight 360s will definitely make the final light dimmer. The best teacher is experimentation.

Fiber optics come in a variety of sizes. I've accumulated many, ranging from some about the thickness of hair taken from an old mood lamp to some as large as the handle of a needle file. By far the most useful have been strands approximately .020″ in diameter. You can find these at science stores, such as American Scientific. One mail order source is Jericho, 601 Linden P1., Evanston, IL 60202.

Fiber optics can also be found in electronics surplus stores and in old mood lamps, which you may spot at a yard sale.

Light sources

The easiest way to transmit light with fiber optics is to position a single bulb next to the end of the fiber in some remote area and then lead the fiber through the layout to its eventual end, in a streetlight for example.

You'll quickly notice that the total usable light will always be limited to the amount of light that strikes the fiber at its initial cross section. This can be enhanced somewhat by beading the end with a flame, as shown in fig. 2. This technique is also called flame-polishing and will improve the performance up to a point. You can also form a bead at the emitting end to create a light bulb shape.

Unless you use an extremely strong light source, fiber optics are poor illuminators, so don't try to use them to light up an area. If you wish to light the inside of a building, the best bet is still grain-of-wheat bulbs or their equivalent. But if you're going to be looking directly at the end of the fiber, the light is strong, clear, and the same color as the source.

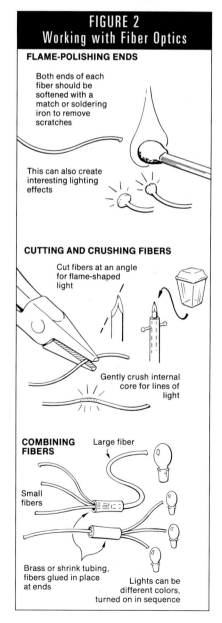

FIGURE 2
Working with Fiber Optics

FLAME-POLISHING ENDS

Both ends of each fiber should be softened with a match or soldering iron to remove scratches

This can also create interesting lighting effects

CUTTING AND CRUSHING FIBERS

Cut fibers at an angle for flame-shaped light

Gently crush internal core for lines of light

COMBINING FIBERS

Large fiber

Small fibers

Brass or shrink tubing, fibers glued in place at ends

Lights can be different colors, turned on in sequence

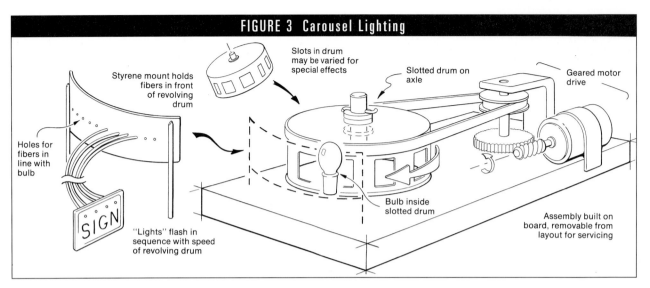

FIGURE 3 Carousel Lighting

Styrene mount holds fibers in front of revolving drum

Slots in drum may be varied for special effects

Slotted drum on axle

Geared motor drive

Holes for fibers in line with bulb

Bulb inside slotted drum

Assembly built on board, removable from layout for servicing

"Lights" flash in sequence with speed of revolving drum

SIGN

FIGURE 4 Aligning Fibers with Bulbs

Insert fibers in ⅛" hole drilled in layout base

Stripwood frame

Fibers in brass tube, glued to frame with epoxy

Align filament with hole

Hold fibers in place with Goo

Bulb mounted above base

Epoxy

Bulb mounted below layout base

Epoxy

MOUNTING FIBERS IN SIGNS

VIEW ANGLE

Complex signs can be combinations of several colors and blinking sequences

Several signs may be illuminated by a single bulb

A Christmas miracle

Prior to last Christmas, I had been working on a method to make lights blink, as shown in fig. 3. I wanted to use this for fiber optics signs, billboards, and such in a city scene. At the time it seemed a good solution. The idea was to periodically block the light reaching the fibers by passing the sides of a slotted cup in front of the source light.

A motor would slowly rotate the cup, and the placement and size of the slots, coordinated with the speed of the rotation, would determine the eventual appearance of the blinking at the end. Of course, if I wanted more than one color I would need one mechanism for each, and any attempt to coordinate the blinking of different colors would be farther out on the technological limb than I cared to venture.

I built three of these contraptions, and then came Christmas. Inspiration is one of the great feelings in life—a bright flash that instantly informs you you've been a dope the whole time. Unfortunately, inspiration can't be developed, nurtured, or rushed. It came when I was looking at a Christmas tree in a store. The lights were blinking in sequence, one after another down the line. Then it hit me! Here was my blinking light source!

I immediately scrapped every bit of complicated machinery on my workbench and began working on the scene you see pictured with this article. As I said, these lights flashed in sequence, with a definite forward motion and an in-line control to determine the tempo. Prior to discovering this product, I thought building

a theater marquee with fiber optic chase lights was possible but just too complicated. But these lights seemed to be the perfect solution.

But there was more! I could change the bulbs. The bulbs are normal Christmas tree twinkle lights avail-

able during the season. The normal sequence for the string was red-green-yellow-blue, but I could make them go red-red-blue-blue, or white-white, or whatever. With this ability I could make signs that go on and off, alternate between colors, or twinkle—any-

58

Fiber optics generate no heat, so they can be mounted in plastic signs with no fear of damage. The light sources can be many feet away. Lee uses strings of blinking Christmas tree lights for special effects.

thing. The potential was beginning to seem endless to me. By this time I had also learned how to combine fibers into bundles, so that the possibilities were verging on the astronomical.

Implementation

The two methods I used with the most success for aligning the fibers with the bulbs are shown in fig. 4. The most important things to remember are that you should have an easy way to change the bulb and that the filament of the bulb should align with the fibers as closely as possible.

When I have aligned the fibers correctly, the light coming out the other end is almost alarmingly bright. I have even found myself thinking that the light must certainly burn out the fiber. This type of thinking comes from years of working with grain-of-wheat bulbs hooked to a transformer and is embarrassingly wrong!

The focal point of the display I

made is the theater marquee. All those lights are really the tips of more than 100 individual fibers, and the effect is exciting. The colored lights march around the perimeter of the sign just as on the real thing.

Each fiber measures .020″ in diameter, although I did flare the end of each just a bit with a match to create a bulb effect and keep the filament from pulling back through the hole. By comparison, the smallest bulb I have ever seen is the Pacific Fast Mail Micro-Miniature, which measures .040″.

Besides being large, bulbs also emit heat, melt plastic, and have two wires that must be hooked up. On the marquee that would mean 200 wires, and then you'd need the electronics to control the sign—but by now I have made my point. With fiber optics construction is a far simpler matter of stringing the fibers through the holes and back to the appropriate bulbs.

Reliability

And now a few words on reliability: Within my pike I also have a string of generic twinkly lights, the kind that have been around for years. The whole string blinks in unison, the pace being set by one master bulb. As with the chase light strings, these are wired by the manufacturer in series, so one bulb going bad means the whole string goes without a hint of where the fault lies.

After approximately 60 hours of operation, one bulb did burn out, followed shortly by another. I blame this mostly on the quality. These strings cost all of $2.50. I was able to find the offending bulbs and replace them and have since wired test leads into these strings to help isolate future problems.

The chase light strings seem to be much more durable. I have yet to experience my first failure after more than 100 hours of operation. The price of these strings (about $20) reflects the additional quality, and I use only the bulbs from other chase light strings in altering colors in the string on the layout.

Ponder the possibilities

Finally there is another idea, which I have not yet worked out but may be of interest to those inventive souls who can't leave the workshop tidy. Consider this: Embedded crushed cores of parallel fibers just below the surface of an Enviro-Tex plastic lake would make sparkling wavelets in the surface. Lead the fibers back to random sparkling white lights, and see what happens. I have already tried this to simulate water running out the end of a pipe, and the result is quite nice. The Enviro-Tex makes the clear portion of the fiber optics disappear.

There's probably a lot more you can do with these miraculous fibers. The sky's the limit, and speaking of skies, how about twinkling stars that come out at night when you turn down the room lights or flashing aircraft warning lights on your taller structures? Just let your imagination roll.

15

Light Up the Night with Neon

By D. Derek Verner
Photos by the author

USING FLUORESCENT PAINT AND
BLACK LIGHT TO MODEL NEON SIGNS

"Neon" signs, colored with fluorescent paint and lit by ultraviolet black light, add life to nighttime scenes.

Neon signs are familiar sights in every city and town. From the sputtering "EATS" sign flickering in the darkness alongside a desolate stretch of highway to the gaudy "Strip" in Las Vegas neon signs have become a traditional part of our landscape. They go further than you might think, as they were introduced in 1910.

Prototype neon signs consist of glass tubing, ¼" to ⅝" in diameter, bent to shape and filled with neon or mixtures of other rare gasses at reduced pressure. Electrodes at the ends of each section of are connected to a high-voltage transformer which causes the gasses to ionize and give

off light. The color of the light is a function of the choice of gasses and color and coating of the tubing.

Modeling neon signs

The best and least expensive way to capture the effect of neon is by using fluorescent paint illuminated by ultraviolet (UV) light. "Black light" lamps like the ones shown in fig. 1 are available from large electrical supply dealers and range in size from a 48", 40-watt unit to a 5¼", 4-watt unit. They operate in a manner similar to fluorescent lamps.

Fixtures for these tubes differ in only one respect from any other fluo-

rescent fixture: The reflector is chrome-plated instead of painted white. The shiny surface redirects UV light from the back side so that it isn't wasted. A painted surface will absorb most of this light. Simply covering the reflector with aluminum duct tape or aluminum foil (shiny side out) will work fine.

Fluorescent paint is available in a wide range of colors. It's sold in craft, hobby, and hardware stores in both spray cans and bottles. I used Testor's fluorescent model paints for most of the signs in the photos. This type of paint appears very bright because it reacts to the UV light present in most

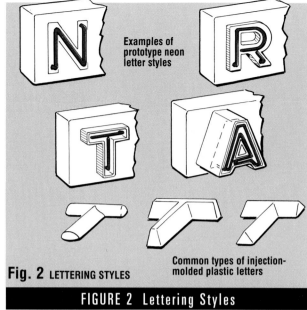

Examples of prototype neon letter styles

Common types of injection-molded plastic letters

Fig. 2 LETTERING STYLES

FIGURE 2 Lettering Styles

Fig. 1. UV LAMPS. "Black Iights" are available in many sizes. The black tubes are designated "BLB," and the white one is designated "BL." Since BL tubes also emit visible light, only BLB lamps are usable for modeling. Commercial black light sources, like the one at left, are not recommended because they produce harmful short-wave UV light as well as the harmless long-wave light produced by the BLB lamps.

light sources. For modeling purposes it makes our signs appear lit even in daylight scenes without UV lamps.

Sources for lettering

Except for small window signs and some skeleton roof signs, most neon signs follow one of the forms shown in fig. 2. This is because businesses want the sign to be visible in daylight as well as at night, when the real impact of neon signs comes across.

At first, the logical way to form model signs appears to be to shape them from thin wire. However, several attempts to do that produced results that I felt were less than successful. The lower "Crown Hotel" sign in fig. 3 shows the results. It's very difficult to form properly proportioned letters by hand. An ideal solution (manufacturers take note) would be to have signs photoetched from suitable artwork.

Using small plastic letters is much easier. Acrylic letters in several colors are available from plastic supply stores. Cast-metal letters are generally not as suitable because they cannot be cemented with plastic solvent.

Several plastic structure kits made for the international market have usable letters. The "Pace Freight," "Wonder Bar," and "Chicago Fruit" signs in fig. 3 came from signs supplied with such kits. Since they're sold in many countries, they frequently include the same words in several languages, offering anagram and Scrabble fans a challenge to see what English words can be made from the letters supplied.

Injection-molded plastic letters usually have one of the three cross sections shown in fig. 2. For modeling, the best shape is the truncated triangle. This is because, in order to mimic the prototype sign formats and reduce the width of the letter strokes, we will light up only the narrow front surface of the letters. Letters with a curved cross section are the least suitable, as they require the entire letter to be illuminated. However, they can be used to model the type of illuminated sign that uses vacuum-formed letters lit from behind by fluorescent tubes.

Letters with a triangular cross section can be used, but it's difficult to paint the sharp front edge. To do this, pour a small puddle of paint on a sheet of glass and dip the letter in so that only the front touches the paint. Another method is to use a fluorescent marking pen, such as the one shown at the upper left of fig. 3. These pens are easier to control than a brush and can coat the sharp edge with ease.

For fluorescent paints to light up brightly they must be applied over a white surface. If the letters are in another color, the area where the fluorescent paint will be applied should first be painted flat white.

Keep your eyes open for swizzle sticks, condiment forks, nameplates, and other items with bas-relief or three-dimensional letters. The "Magic Pan," "Westinghouse," "Garrard," "McDonald's," "Marriot," and "Lady Baltimore" signs in fig. 3 are from such sources.

Figure 4 shows several typical sign designs. Skeleton roof signs generally have some sort of grid or framework to which the sign is affixed. The "Lady Baltimore" sign in fig 3 was mounted on a Grandt Line window casting, and the hand-formed "Crown Hotel" sign was mounted on a frame made from Plastruct angle pieces. The other "Crown Hotel" sign is mounted on a piece of wire screen. The solder blobs at the intersections of the wires can be filed down, if they seem objectionable.

Letters mounted against a wall, such as "Lulu's Lunchroom" and "Lacy's Variety" are simply cemented to an appropriately colored background, as are the projection and upright sign letters.

Other materials

Fluorescent paper, shown in fig. 3, is available from art supply stores. The paper can be used as glowing backgrounds for signs in which the lettering is done with black dry-transfer letters. That's how the lower half of the "Chilb Lanes" bowling alley sign was done. One way to make window and other signs is to use the paper (or the paint) behind a Kodalith negative, like the "Tony's Fruits and Vegetables" and "Lehman" signs in fig. 3. (The high-contrast Kodalith film is available from large photography stores; professional photographers or graphic artists can also shoot these from your prepared artwork.)

Make sure the paper is in tight contact with the negative, or this technique won't work properly. Place

Fig. 3. MATERIALS. These common materials take on new life when they're exposed to black light.

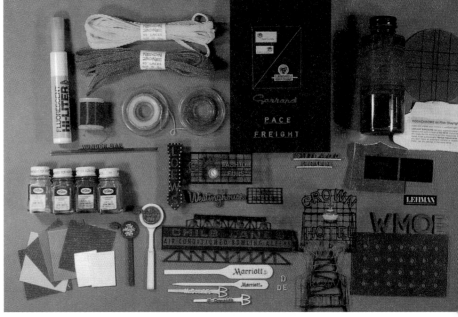

Fig.4 TYPICAL SMALL SIGNS

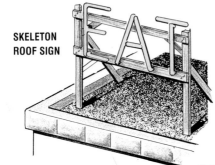

SKELETON ROOF SIGN

WALL AND WINDOW SIGNS

Fig. 5 LIGHTING A SMALL AREA

Black light hidden inside building, out of view of operator

PROJECTION SIGN

UPRIGHT SIGN

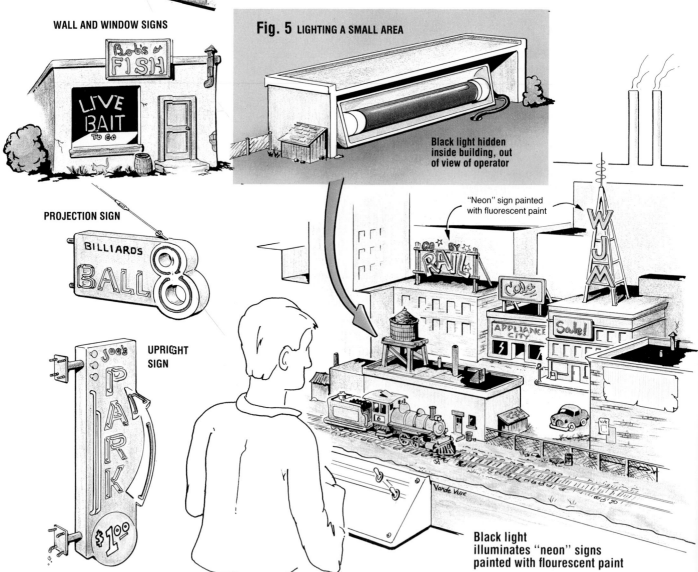

"Neon" sign painted with fluorescent paint

Black light illuminates "neon" signs painted with flourescent paint

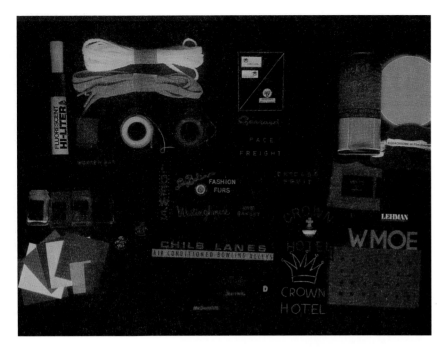

small dots of Walthers Goo or contact cement on the opaque areas of the negative to bind it closely to the paper.

Decals can be mounted on fluorescent paper if the decal carrier film is the full size of the backing paper. Decals not made this way won't work well because the edge of the decal film will be visible. The "Lorie's Gifts" sign illustrates this method. Before applying the decal, spray the paper with a sealant such as Testor's Glosscote.

Many art supply stores carry fluorescent dry-transfer letters. The upper half of the "Chilb Lanes" sign was made using these. Even though the letters have an under-printing of white pigment, they work better if mounted on a light but contrasting color background rather than the dark one shown. Note that this sign is supposedly frontlit by floodlights. This technique works as well for signs supposedly backlit.

Another way of modeling a sign lit by floodlights is to use a transparent liquid called Living Light. Figure 3 shows this product next to a film box that's been given a coat of it. Notice that the painted area lights up brightly and the printed lettering shows through. Living Light can be applied to any surface, causing it to light up under UV light. It can be used for signs or to create puddles of light around dummy streetlights. Living Light (stock no. A-810) is distributed by Ultra-Violet Products, San Gabriel, CA 91776.

Ordinary paper, including many signs offered by model suppliers, is sometimes fluorescent without special treatment. Two rectangles of typing paper are shown on top of the color swatches in fig. 3. One glows brightly under UV, the other does not. That's because manufacturers often put fluorescent dyes into products to make them appear whiter and brighter.

You may be surprised at how many products around the house glow under the influence of UV light. This can be a drawback if you use UV lighting on your layout. You may find that some of your modeling materials glow brightly when you don't want them to. If this happens, you may have to repaint the item in non-fluorescent paint. Some dealers in UV products market a transparent liquid that will stop the transmission of UV light so the item no longer glows.

Other fluorescent items shown in fig. 3 include elastic, thread, yarn, and shoelaces. All the fluorescent fabric materials I've seen are made of fine filaments that are bundled together. These can be unraveled and regrouped into bundles as thin as you like. They're excellent for modeling straight lengths of neon tubing to outline signs or serve as accent lighting on movie marquees. The lines shown on the piece of construction paper were made this way. Fluorescent drafting tape (as narrow as ½″) is also available.

Some plastics are available in fluorescent colors, and fig. 3 shows some acrylic pieces and molded letters. The letters are large for most purposes, but they work well for call letters mounted atop a broadcasting station.

Placing the UV lamps

If you plan to use fluorescent materials extensively on your layout, you may want to flood an entire scene with UV light by suspending large (40-watt) fixtures overhead. If you do, be sure to take full advantage of the benefits of UV by using the pigments and materials for other lighting effects. How about stars and a glowing moon for your night sky? You could light street lamps, vehicle and train lights, and windows. Even the windows in flat backgrounds can be lighted with paint or small squares of fluorescent paper.

If you want to light only a few signs or areas, the smaller-sized lamps can be concealed within or behind other structures as shown in fig. 5. Remember that these lights operate on 110 volts and should be wired accordingly.

Try some of the techniques outlined in this article. When visitors admire your handiwork, you can be assured that it's a good sign.

16

Painted Power

By D. Derek Verner
Photos by the author

USE CONDUCTIVE PAINT TO LIGHT UP FIGURES AND DETAILS

Conductive paint lets you light up these details without wires.

Imagine being able to add lighting to details and accessories without having to worry about concealing wires. Conductive paint, a metal-bearing paint used in the electronics industry for repairing PC boards, lets us do just that.

Getting started

Several sources for LEDs, lamps, and conductive paints are listed in the accompanying table. The Circuit Works pen in fig. 1, made by Planned Products, is about the handiest source of conductive paint. It is available from many electronics dealers. You can contact Planned Products (see the table for information) to

find a local distributor or order direct.

Let's start by providing illumination to the three-piece styrene lampposts made by Campbell, shown in fig. 2. Figure 3 shows how to do it. The terminal posts offer a means of mounting and supply power to the lamppost. Heat the brass rods at one end before pressing them into the holes. This creates a firm mechanical connection. Trim off the protruding nipple at the top of the mast and cut notches with a hobby knife as shown.

I've found the Cir-Kit Concepts 1.5-volt lamps work very well. They have insulated flexible leads that must be removed for use here. Since the lamp is so tiny, it can easily get lost.

To prevent this, wrap the glass envelope with a temporary handle of masking tape.

Use a soldering iron to carefully unsolder the bulb. The insulating material at the base of the bulb will also soften with the heat. To make sure you don't short out the wires by inadvertently soldering them together, spread the leads in opposite directions and apply tension while unsoldering them. Clean the rest of the insulating material from the wires. Bend the wires as shown in fig. 3, and use five-minute epoxy to secure them in the notches. Place the clear lantern head in position and allow the adhesive to cure. Examine the head of the lamppost; if necessary, scrape off excess epoxy covering the surface of the wires. As fig. 1 shows, paint a trace of conductive pigment from each wire of the bulb to one of the brass rods in the base. The paint usually flows well. If you experience difficulty, unscrew the head and dip a small paintbrush into the pen's reservoir. You can make the traces as wide as you like, but be sure to keep them from touching one another. Test the assembly by applying 1.5 volts to the rods. If all is well, finish the lamppost by painting it the color of your choice.

The other plastic lamppost shown in the photos is one supplied in a number of structure kits. I treated it in a similar fashion, except I cut off the globe. I replaced it with a miniature bulb and topped it with a punched-out metal disk.

Metal lampposts

Metal castings, such as the Scale Structures Ltd. lamppost, can also be used. The casting itself serves as one conductor to the lamp and, after an insulating coat of paint, the second conductor is painted on.

Add one brass rod terminal as with the plastic post. As fig. 3 shows, drill a second hole, insert a length of toothpick, and secure it in place with epoxy. This, when coated with conductive paint, will serve as the second input terminal.

File a notch on one side of the globe base and solder one lead from the lamp into the depression, as shown in fig. 3. Paint the entire lamppost casting with an acrylic paint, such as Polly S, and give the other lead from the lamp several coats as well. Allow the paint to dry thoroughly and glue the painted lead into the notch with epoxy cement.

The paint should insulate the wire from the casting. Check to see that this is the case by scraping the paint (and any epoxy) from the outer surface of the wire and testing it with an ohmmeter. There should be a few ohms of resistance (the bulb) between the brass terminal rod and the scraped portion of the painted wire lead.

If the resistance checks out, apply a trace of conductive paint from the scraped lead down to and covering the toothpick. Finish the lamp as with the plastic one. For the lamp in the photos I added a plastic-bead globe

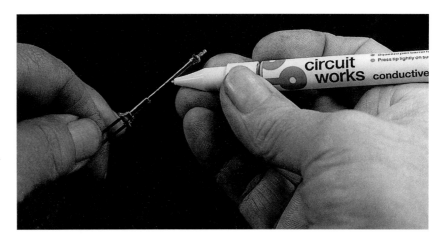

Fig. 1. PAINTING A PATH. The Circuit Works conductive pen is the easiest way to apply the conductive paint to details.

Fig. 2. COMMERCIAL DETAILS. Various brands and types of metal and plastic lampposts can be illuminated using conductive paints. The light sources shown at right include a standard LED, Hewlett Packard low-current LED, Cir-Kit Concepts miniature bulb, and two other small bulbs.

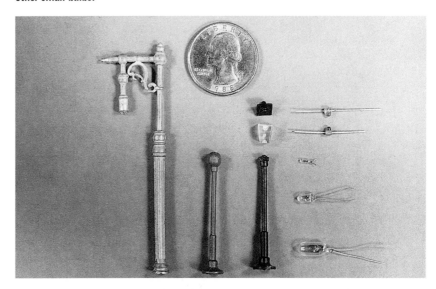

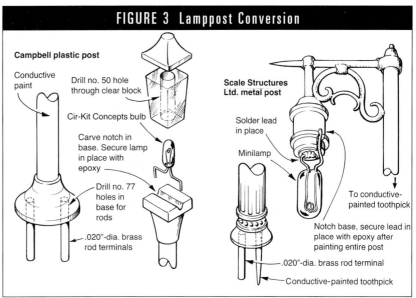

FIGURE 3 Lamppost Conversion

Campbell plastic post

Conductive paint

Drill no. 50 hole through clear block

Cir-Kit Concepts bulb

Carve notch in base. Secure lamp in place with epoxy

Drill no. 77 holes in base for rods

.020"-dia. brass rod terminals

Scale Structures Ltd. metal post

Solder lead in place

Minilamp

To conductive-painted toothpick

Notch base, secure lead in place with epoxy after painting entire post

.020"-dia. brass rod terminal

Conductive-painted toothpick

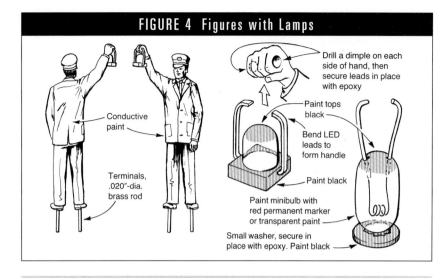

FIGURE 4 Figures with Lamps

Conductive paint

Terminals, .020"-dia. brass rod

Drill a dimple on each side of hand, then secure leads in place with epoxy

Paint tops black

Bend LED leads to form handle

Paint black

Paint minibulb with red permanent marker or transparent paint

Small washer, secure in place with epoxy. Paint black

SOURCES FOR MATERIALS

Circuit Works conductive pen, a silverbearing paint in an applicator, designed for repairing PC traces. Manufactured by Planned Products, 21105 Santa Cruz Hwy., Brush Rd., Los Gatos, CA 95030; 408-459-8088.

Nickel Print (part no. S1199-105, 22-207), a nickel-bearing conductive paint with a conductivity of 5 to 6 ohms per square centimeter, and **Silver Print** (part no. S8426-105, 22-201), a silverbearing conductive paint with a conductivity of 0.1 ohms per square centimeter, are made by GC Electronics and sold by Edlie Electronics, 2700 Hempstead Tnpk., Levittown, NY 11765.

J. C. Whitney & Co., offers a copper-bearing repair kit (part no. 14-7961P) for automobile electric rear window defrosters. The conductivity is better than nickel, but not as good as silver. The kit is sold by J. C. Whitney & Co., 1917-19 Archer Ave., P. O. Box 8410, Chicago, IL 60680.

Hewlett Packard subminiature 5V, 4mA LED, (part no. HLMP-6620), sold by R&D Electronics (stock no. 385F7), 1224 Prospect Ave., Cleveland, OH 44116.

Cir-Kit Concepts Inc. 1.5V, 15mA Micro-lamps (part nos. CK-1010-13, black wires, and CK-101-14, white wires), sold by Cir-Kit Concepts Inc., 407 14th St. N.W., Rochester, MN 55901 (also available from Wm. K. Walthers).

taken from a dime-store necklace. I drilled it out and slipped it over the exposed bulb.

Figures

These principles can be applied to flashlights and lanterns held by your layout's miniature inhabitants. The fellow in the photo on page 102 who's holding a small boy by the scruff of the neck and holding a lighted flashlight in his left hand is the usher from my Lido Theater (March 1976 *Model Railroader*). Figure 4 shows how to do it. Insert a brass rod into each foot of the figure and prepare the bulb or LED by bending the leads as shown.

LEDs and miniature lamps

Many types of miniature and subminiature lamps and LEDs are suitable for use with painted power. Of interest are low-current LEDs, which I used for all the hand lanterns. These LEDs draw only 4 milliamps, compared to the 30 to 40 of an average LED. Narrow painted traces, particularly nickel or copper paint, can't carry much current without heating up, so the small current requirement is a bonus. These LEDs are designed to operate on 5 volts, but a dropping resistor should be used if operated at a higher-than-rated voltage. A 1.8K-ohm resistor in series with the LED will light it at close to its rated current on 12 volts.

The other subminiature LED that's shown in fig. 2 is an ordinary type, requiring a dropping resistor. Its base, however, is round and may look more like a railroad lantern.

The smallest lamp in fig. 2 is the CirKit Concepts bulb after its leads have been unsoldered. The others are available from electronics surplus houses such as R&D Electronics. They're available in many different sizes and voltage ratings and are much less expensive than lamps bought in a hobby shop. Miniature 50- and 100-lamp Christmas tree strings are excellent sources of low-voltage miniature lamps. If you wait until the post-holiday sales, you can get a bargain. They have pointed tips that make them unsuitable for some purposes, but the price is right.

Both LEDs and incandescent lamps can be operated on AC or DC, but I prefer AC for two reasons. First, all other things being equal, incandescent lamps have a longer life on AC. Second, low-voltage transformers are cheaper than DC power supplies.

Power to the people

All that remains is to deliver the required power to the brass terminals. I drill appropriately sized and spaced holes in the terrain, insert the rods, and solder feeder wires from under the layout. If you choose this method, be sure to use some sort of heatsink or the plastic may deform. A close examination of the figure with the lantern at his side will show what looks like a club foot—I didn't use a heatsink.

An alternative is to use small alligator clips. Use the insulated ones such as those available from Radio Shack. This will allow you to remove the item for servicing or place it in a new location. Clips are also easy to use, which is important since soldering to a silver-coated toothpick or sprue is difficult at best. Another option is to recess small pieces of brass tubing into your terrain, forming plug-in sockets.

Whatever your choice, be sure to try painted power for people, signal heads, vehicles, lampposts, and whatever else your imagination can dream up.

17

Landscape Lighting

By Mark Grossetti
Photo by Rich Muller

EASY TECHNIQUES TO SIMULATE REALISTIC
OUTDOOR RESIDENTIAL LIGHTING

Garage light, front-porch light, yardlight—even sidewalk
lights! Is this suburbia at dusk, or what? Hope someone
remembers to close the garage door at bedtime.

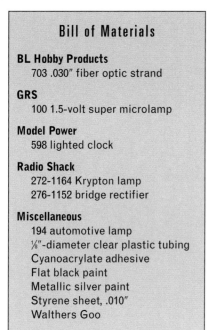

Bill of Materials

BL Hobby Products
703 .030″ fiber optic strand

GRS
100 1.5-volt super microlamp

Model Power
598 lighted clock

Radio Shack
272-1164 Krypton lamp
276-1152 bridge rectifier

Miscellaneous
194 automotive lamp
⅛″-diameter clear plastic tubing
Cyanoacrylate adhesive
Flat black paint
Metallic silver paint
Styrene sheet, .010″
Walthers Goo

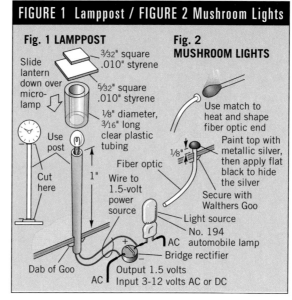

FIGURE 1 Lamppost / FIGURE 2 Mushroom Lights

Fig. 1 LAMPPOST

Slide lantern down over micro-lamp

³⁄₃₂″ square .010″ styrene

⁵⁄₃₂″ square .010″ styrene

⅛″ diameter, ³⁄₁₆″ long clear plastic tubing

Use post

Cut here

1″

Fiber optic

Wire to 1.5-volt power source

Dab of Goo

AC

Output 1.5 volts
Input 3-12 volts AC or DC

Fig. 2 MUSHROOM LIGHTS

Use match to heat and shape fiber optic end

Paint top with metallic silver, then apply flat black to hide the silver

⅛″

Secure with Walthers Goo

Light source

No. 194 automobile lamp

AC

Bridge rectifier

By themselves little HO scale yard lights don't seem like much, but once they're installed and working you'll be pleasantly surprised. Their tiny pools of light add a touch of realism that's sure to capture any visitor's attention.

Lamppost

Commercial streetlights are far too large to simulate the decorative lampposts found in many front yards. I use the decorative post from a Model Power clock or other similar lighted accessory by removing the original lamp and trimming off the top and bottom as in fig. 1.

Drop the wires from a 1.5-volt microlamp through the post until the glass rests on the top end. Cut a piece of clear plastic tubing to fit over the lamp and simulate the glass housing. Add a cap made from bits of styrene, secured with cyanoacrylate adhesive (CA). Paint the "cast iron" parts flat black.

Put a tiny drop of Walthers Goo on top of the lamp and slip the housing over it. Drill a snug mounting hole in the layout, thread the wires through it, and press the post into place so it's between 6 and 8 feet tall.

Wire it to a 1.5-volt power supply. I use one published in Bill Defoe's article in the July 1991 *Model Railroader.* Its wiring diagram is shown in fig. 1.

Low path lights

My low mushroom-shaped path or garden lights are made from fiber optics. Use a match to heat the end of a single .030″ fiber so it flares out into a mushroom shape.

Allow it to cool and then paint the top metallic silver to reflect the light downward. See fig. 2. After the silver hardens, paint the top of the housing flat black.

Drill a row of close-fitting holes along the path and slip the fiber optic ends through them. Adjust the height so each lamp is about a scale foot high and secure it with a drop of Walthers Goo.

Bundle the fibers together and use a clear lamp to supply the brightest light possible. I recommend using the 7.2-volt Krypton flashlight lamp sold by Radio Shack.

18

Bishop's Crook Station Lamps

By Bill Rooke
Photo by the author

EASY-TO-BUILD HO WORKING LIGHTS FOR YOUR LAYOUT

The lamps lining this HO station platform
were scratchbuilt according to techniques
described in this article.

These graceful HO scale station lamps are patterned after those that once stood on the open north platform of the Delaware & Hudson station at Plattsburgh, N. Y. The station has since been converted to a restaurant, but you can still see the lamps, as they were refurbished and relocated to the sidewalk along the front of the structure. Building a set of lamps will take one or two evenings. This project lends itself nicely to mass production.

The mast

Consult fig. 1 and bend a piece of .020″ brass rod into a U shape for the mast. I bent mine around a ¼″ stove bolt clamped in a bench vise. Cut the short side to proper length, but leave about 2″ extra on the long side to extend below the layout surface.

To make the scrollwork you'll need a jig like the one shown in fig. 2. Any scrap of soft wood will work fine for this. The wires and nails you stick in need be only about ½″ long.

Now start scrolling, using a single strand from a piece of no. 18 lamp cord and following the winding pattern included in fig. 2. Keep all the loops tight, especially the first and last.

Using a sharp pointed tool such as a modeling knife, gently lift the scrollwork off the jig and lay it on the workbench. Solder or connect the wires with cyanoacrylate adhesive (CA) wherever they touch each other.

I prefer to solder. First I tin the soldering tool by melting a small amount of solder on the tip. Then I apply a very small amount of rosin-base soldering paste (flux) to each location where the wires cross or touch. I just touch the connection, and enough solder will flow from the iron to make the connection.

If solder fills in the small holes, reheat the connection and use the point of a toothpick or a solder-removing braid (available from Radio Shack) to remove the excess. Too much rosin won't usually create a problem except in cleaning up.

When the soldering is complete, trim the excess wire flush with the circles. Tin the inside of the crook. At the three points where the scrollwork will touch, apply a small amount of rosin. Place the scroll and heat the contact points. The rosin should draw enough solder from the tinned crook to attach the scroll. If not, melt a little

more solder onto the soldering tool and reheat.

The bulb

The key to the success of this project is the microbulbs available from Cir-Kit Concepts, 407 14th St. N. W., Rochester, MN 55901. These bulbs, however, come with a length of stranded wire that's too heavy for our use and must be removed. The question is, how?

Mike Evans of Plattsburgh Hobbies had the answer. Cut the wire about ½″ or so from the bulb. Soak the bulb in a bottle of liquid plastic cement for two or three hours (overnight is even better). This will soften the insulation to a point that it can be removed with your fingers or tweezers. A small, thin layer of harder plastic will remain, but you can scrape it off with a modeling knife.

To hold the bulb, insert it into a piece of insulation from no. 18 gauge lamp cord. Working over a white surface for better vision, examine the bulb under magnification; you'll see that each wire is connected to a small, single-wire "pigtail." Heat one of these connections, and remove the stranded wire.

Tin the pigtail, using rosin and touching solder to it, then bring the pigtail into contact with the short end of the crook. Apply heat, and solder the bulb to the post.

From this point on, test the lamp with a 1.5-volt battery after each procedure to avoid a lot of useless work.

Cut a piece of 36AWG magnet

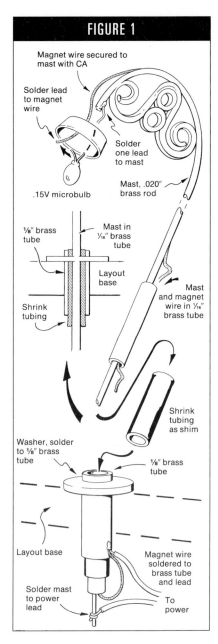

FIGURE 1

Magnet wire secured to mast with CA

Solder lead to magnet wire

Solder one lead to mast

.15V microbulb

Mast, .020″ brass rod

⅛″ brass tube

Mast in ¹⁄₁₆″ brass tube

Layout base

Shrink tubing

Mast and magnet wire in ¹⁄₁₆″ brass tube

Shrink tubing as shim

Washer, solder to ⅛″ brass tube

⅛″ brass tube

Layout base

Magnet wire soldered to brass tube and lead

Solder mast to power lead

To power

wire so it's 2″ longer than is needed to reach the bottom of the post. (My magnet wire comes from Newark Electronics, 500 N. Pulaski Rd., Chicago, IL 60624.) Scrape a bit of the insulating enamel off one end of the wire and tin it.

Remove the stranded wire from the bulb's other pigtail and tin it. Carefully solder the magnet wire to it. After checking the electrical connection, put a bit of paint on each of the bulb's pigtails to insulate them. Set aside to dry.

Finishing the post

Carefully route the magnet wire along the crook of the lamppost, attaching it with CA. Route the wire through a piece of ¹⁄₁₆″ brass tubing,

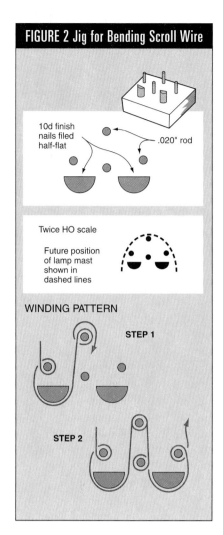

FIGURE 2 Jig for Bending Scroll Wire

10d finish
nails filed
half-flat

.020" rod

Twice HO scale

Future position
of lamp mast
shown in
dashed lines

WINDING PATTERN

STEP 1

STEP 2

and slide the tubing over the lamppost to simulate the larger-diameter pipe at the bottom of the post. Secure with CA, and then test electrical continuity. (If the lamp doesn't work, make sure you removed a little insulation from the end of the magnet wire.)

Cut a piece of ⅛" brass tubing long enough to go through your layout base. Drill or file out a small brass washer until it slips snugly over the tubing.

Now drill a ⅛" perpendicular hole in a piece of pine. It can be the same piece used for the scroll form. Set the assembly in the wood to square the washer with the tube. Leaving about 1/16" of tube above the washer, run a solder fillet around the brass tube to form a base for the lamppost.

Slip a piece of heat-shrink tubing over the 1/16" brass tubing on the lamppost. Slide the base of the lamp over the insulated tubing, even with the bottom of the model, and secure with CA.

Lamp shades

I made shades from headlight lenses for Athearn's PA-1 locomotive. First I drilled a 1/16" hole straight through the lens, then I reamed out the inside with a sharp ¼" drill held in my fingers. This provided a nice

reflector of a more modern style. You could also use commercial shades from Grandt Line or Campbell.

Last I painted the lamp black as per the prototype, You could also use green or silver.

Using the wire that was clipped from the bulb earlier in the project, solder one piece to the rod sticking out of the brass tubing. See fig. 1. Solder the other piece and the free end of the magnet wire to the ⅛" brass tubing. It provides a more stable support for the rather delicate wire. Drill a 5/32" hole in the layout to provide a mounting place for the lamp. Hook up the lamp to a 1.5-volt power source and enjoy.

How to Simulate Flickering Fires

By D. Derek Verner
Photos by the author

THESE EASY-TO-BUILD CIRCUITS ARE POWERED BY AN OLD RADIO

Workers at a junkyard are warming themselves by burning trash in a 55-gallon oil drum. The flickering flames add a nice touch.

The ancient Greeks believed that everything in the world was composed of four basic elements: air, earth, water, and fire. In model railroading we needn't concern ourselves with modeling air since it can't be seen. As for earth and water, there have been countless articles on modeling these, but very few on simulating fire.

As an electronics hobbyist I have long sought a simple circuit that produces random voltage changes which could be used to imitate the flicker of a flame.

The basic concept

One day as I was troubleshooting a stereo system with an oscilloscope, the solution hit me. As I watched the audio signals on the scope, I suddenly realized that the circuit I was seeking was probably in every home in America! The output of an ordinary radio is about as random (at least visually) as anything is going to get.

Almost any radio can be used—AM or FM, transistorized or tube type—as long as it has sufficient output to drive a loudspeaker. It doesn't even have to be working perfectly; if it has bad filter capacitors and an annoying 60-cycle hum or lots of static—so much the better, as we shall see later.

Many radios have a mini jack installed that permits an external speaker or a pair of headphones to be plugged in. The jack has a built-in switch that cuts off the signals to the speaker and, instead, feeds them to the plug. If you're using one of these radios, all you have to do is insert a mini plug connected to a small lamp, tune to a strong station, and watch the lamp flicker.

At normal listening levels, most radios put out about 3 or 4 volts RMS (root-mean-square), so any small 5- or 6-volt lamp should work. You can adjust the overall brightness by means of the volume control. Start with it turned down all the way and bring it up gradually to avoid burning out the lamp.

In some radios there's a resistor in the circuit that cuts down the level of the signal to prevent damage to earphones. This will keep your flame from burning brightly. You can easily bypass this resistor. Open up the radio (if it operates on 110 volts, be sure it's unplugged) and check to see if there is a resistor in the circuit between the jack and the speaker. If

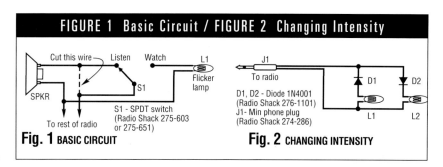

FIGURE 1 Basic Circuit / FIGURE 2 Changing Intensity

Fig. 1 BASIC CIRCUIT

Fig. 2 CHANGING INTENSITY

so, short it out with a wire jumper; this will bring the output up to speaker level.

If the radio has no jack, you can disconnect the speaker wires and extend them outside the radio to power your lamp. You may even want to install a switch as shown in fig. 1 so you can listen to your favorite station or power your fire simulation circuit. The basic circuit in fig. 1 works fine for small fires such as campfires and gas lamps.

Moving flames

So much for the basic idea. There are a few refinements that may be of use in special applications. One of the qualities of flames is that they not only constantly change in intensity, but seem to move back and forth as well. If we were to use two lamps and cause them to reach peak brightness at different times, we could produce the desired effect.

Since the audio signal is AC, we can do this by using two small diodes connected as shown in fig. 2. When the signal goes positive, one lamp will light; when it goes negative, the other will.

Because LEDs are diodes, you can use them in place of the diode/lamp combination shown in fig. 2. Connect two diodes in parallel, anode to cathode, and apply your audio signal. If they fail to light or light only dimly, try placing an 8- or 10-ohm resistor in parallel with them.

One problem with LEDs is that they are monochromatic; therefore, you can't use filters to change their color. However, amber LEDs aren't too far from the color of fire, and their life is much longer than incandescent lamps. Note that no series dropping resistors are required because there isn't enough current available to damage them.

Small flames

How can you model a tiny flame, like a handheld torch or a figure

lighting a cigarette? I use the micro-bulbs sold by Cir-Kit Concepts (407 14th St. N. W., Rochester, MN 55901; 507-288-0860). These tiny bulbs operate on 1.5 volts and quickly burn out at higher voltages. Even with the volume control set to minimum, just turning the radio on or off can cause a spike that will burn one out.

If you want to drive a Cir-Kit lamp, use the arrangement shown in fig. 3. It can easily be built on a small piece of perfboard as shown. The circuit uses the voltage drop across two pairs of diodes to limit the maximum voltage the lamp can receive, regardless of the volume control setting.

Each diode drops about .7 volt, so two in series come to about 1.4 volts —perfect for use with the microbulb. Since the voltage is AC, two pairs must be used to protect the lamp when the signal goes positive or negative. With this setup, the voltage across the lamp can go from 0 to 1.4 volts, but no higher.

Neon lamps

Another way to simulate a fire is to use an NE2 neon lamp or its brighter cousin the NE2H (both available from Radio Shack). The color of ionized neon is a pretty good approximation of the color of fire. A neon lamp operating on AC flickers back and forth automatically. There's no filament in these lamps, just two electrodes in a glass envelope filled with neon gas. The lamp acts like an open circuit until the voltage rises high enough to ionize the gas.

If the voltage is DC, the gas around only one electrode lights. If it's AC, the gas around each electrode lights alternately. On 60 hertz this happens 120 times a second; so fast that it appears both are lit. With a constantly varying audio signal, the flashing back and forth is quite obvious.

The neon doesn't ionize until a voltage of about 90 volts is reached. Since we have an output of only 3 or 4

FIGURE 3 Small Bulbs for Small Flames / FIGURE 4 Neon Lamp Circuit

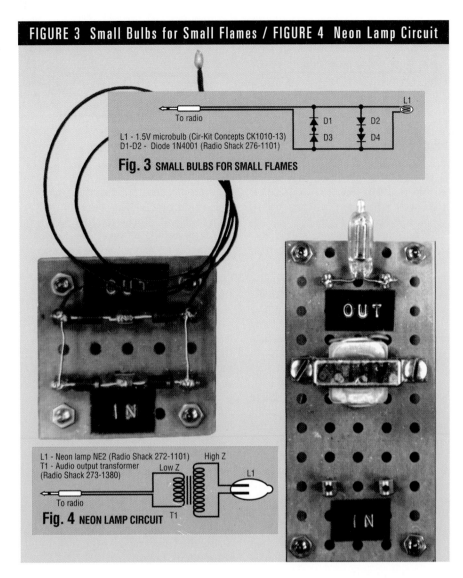

Fig. 3 SMALL BULBS FOR SMALL FLAMES

L1 - 1.5V microbulb (Cir-Kit Concepts CK1010-13)
D1-D2 - Diode 1N4001 (Radio Shack 276-1101)

L1 - Neon lamp NE2 (Radio Shack 272-1101)
T1 - Audio output transformer (Radio Shack 273-1380)

Fig. 4 NEON LAMP CIRCUIT

volts, we need a method of increasing this to more than 90 volts. The circuit in fig. 4 will do that easily, using what's called an audio output transformer.

We're using it connected in reverse as a voltage step-up transformer to take the low-voltage signal and boost it to several hundred volts. Even though the voltage is high, there isn't any danger of a shock. You'd have to wet your fingers to even feel it. That's because the signal is almost all voltage and almost no current. However, it does drive the neon lamp to give off a brilliant flickering effect that's much brighter than it would be if operating on the 110-volt line.

I'm not recommending it, but if these neon lamps were operated from 110-volt house mains, a high-value series resistor would be required to prevent the lamp from being destroyed. Once the gas is ionized, it becomes an excellent conductor and, unless the current flow is limited, the lamp will explode. In our circuit, no limiting resistor is required because there isn't enough current available to damage the lamp.

Adjusting the flicker

Regardless of which of the circuits you decide to use, the procedure for adjustment is the same. Start with lis-tening to the radio by pulling the earphone plug or flipping the switch if you installed one. Find a strong station, turn down the volume, and switch back to the fire effect. Advance the volume control slowly until the lamp starts to flicker. Some stations give better results than others; try rock 'n roll as well as classical music. See what gives the best effect.

If the lamp goes completely off for too long, try tuning off frequency slightly. It may sound terrible, but it does fill in the valleys and keep the home fires burning.

I've found that FM, without the muting switch turned on, produces a nice white noise when the station isn't tuned in precisely. Be sure to find a 24-hour-a-day station, or you may find that the Eternal Flame in front of the Casey Jones Memorial Shrine goes out at night.

Modeling flames

So far I've described only the electrical part of the fire effect. How can we model the actual flame? That depends on what the flame represents. Is it a blast furnace, a barbecue pit, or a forest fire?

The lead photo shows some junkyard workers warming themselves by burning trash in a 55-gallon oil drum. This uses two bulbs painted yellow with touches of Testor's orange transparent paint. The bulbs, powered from beneath the layout, are located in the drum, which is made from a length of metal tubing. A small piece of plastic from a white translucent supermarket shopping bag is inserted into the top of the drum in much the same way a handkerchief is tucked into a breast pocket. As the lamps flicker, the plastic takes on different colors. You could even add a Seuthe smoke generator.

In some cases, a burning building for example, you might not see the flames directly, but only the flickering yellow and orange light visible through the windows. Use your imagination. I hope that some of these ideas will help to light a fire under you.

20

Pole Lights for a Freight Yard

By John Licharson
Photos by the author

Use them to mark uncoupling ramps and
"enlighten" your operators

Those scratchbuilt lights look good and are inexpensive. You could probably build a dozen in one evening.

Here's a quick and easy project for your HO layout. You can use these working pole lights in a freight yard, as I did, or anywhere else. All you need are typing paper, some miniature bulbs, and a few minutes time.

Actually, my lights grew out of the desire to solve a problem that had nothing at all to do with lighting. My Kaministiquia freight yard includes six closely spaced parallel tracks, so the view of the Kadee magnets on five of them was usually blocked by cars on closer tracks.

A friend had marked the centers of his uncoupling ramps with ties painted yellow or posts. That would not work for me, though, as my layout is high (42"), making the viewing angle too low. His example, though, did give me an idea.

Yards often have lights, and these lights have to be higher than the cars to be of any practical use. Ergo: I could mark magnet locations with light poles.

Bulbs & shades

The first step is to make conical shades for the lights, as shown in fig. 1. For this you need a stiff but thin paper, such as medium bond. Fold the paper to make a bunch of shades all at the same time, then drill through the stack with a ¹⁄₃₂" drill. Go carefully to make sure the hole is clean.

Next, center the die part of a paper punch on the hole and punch through, producing a bunch of little paper disks with neatly centered holes. Now with a modeling knife, cut a slit from the hole to the outer edge of each disk.

Next attach the shades to the bulbs. This is rather like wrapping a towel around yourself after a shower. Overlap the edges of the disk until the conical shape is achieved and hold it in place with tweezers. Carefully apply cyanoacrylate adhesive (CA) to the "waist"—just enough to hold the cone to the bulb without also gluing on the tweezers.

Once the glue has set, you can hold the bulb by the lead wires and apply more CA to make a smoother top side of the shade. (An even simpler way of doing this is to buy Micro-Lighting bulbs with shades already attached.)

Conductive poles

Make the poles from ¹⁄₁₆" brass or copper tubing, as shown in fig. 2. The idea is to simulate wooden poles similar to telephone poles. Cut the tubing to length, the correct length being the desired height of the pole, plus ½" for mounting. I used 4½".

With a file, round the edges at the top so they won't cut the insulation on the wire you insert later. Then file a flat spot at the butt end. Put a small bit of solder on the flat spot and also tin a spot ¼" from the top of the pole.

Carefully bend the bulb leads to a right angle. Bend too hard or too fast and you'll break one or both. Check to make sure the light still works. I

FIGURE 1 Making Lamp Shades / FIGURE 2 Adding Lights to Poles

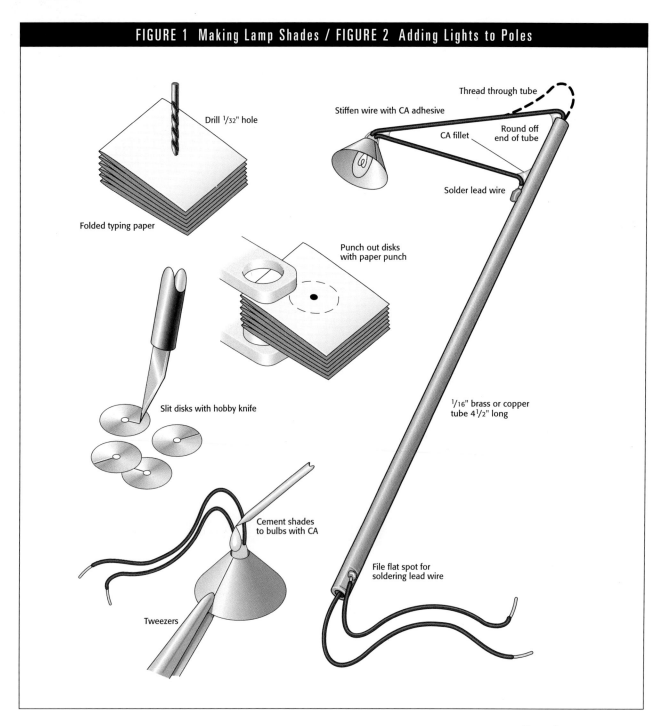

Drill $^1/_{32}$" hole

Folded typing paper

Punch out disks with paper punch

Slit disks with hobby knife

Cement shades to bulbs with CA

Tweezers

Thread through tube

Stiffen wire with CA adhesive

CA fillet

Round off end of tube

Solder lead wire

$^1/_{16}$" brass or copper tube $4^1/_2$" long

File flat spot for soldering lead wire

touch the leads to a 1.5-volt battery.

Next, cut one of the leads ⅝" from the bend. Solder the piece you've just cut off to the flat spot on the bottom of the pole. Remove the insulation from the last ⅛" of the short wire lead and solder that to the tinned part at the top of the pole. Thread the other wire lead down through the top, taking care not to strip any insulation.

Gently pull the two leads so the wires are straight and form a right angle with the top part of the pole. Fix and stiffen the wires with a light "painting" of CA. The result is a lamp bracket formed by the bulb's lead wires.

Paint the shade and bracket a rusty black. Paint the pole brown for a creosoted wood pole, or use the appropriate colors if you want concrete or metal. For these latter you could fashion a square base from plastic, drilling a hole that would allow it to be slipped on before soldering the lead wires.

Let the pole dry thoroughly before drilling a ⅟₁₆" hole and installing it.

Postscript

For additional detail, you can attach a guy wire about three-quarters of the way up the pole, with the other end planted in the ground a short distance away. I've also painted a yellow band high on the pole to help my operators even more in finding those magnets.

That's all there is to it. Once you get started on this project you can probably think of a lot more places on your layout to add these quick and easy lights.

21

A Carload of Sound

By D. Derek Verner
Photos by the author

An inexpensive onboard sound system that
lets you record your own effects

Derek Verner used Memo-Mate message recorders to build
sound systems for these two cars. The circuit board is visible behind the open boxcar door. The hopper has a speaker
at each end.

How would you like to have an onboard sound system that can duplicate the sounds produced by any train ever built? You can even include the mooing of the cattle traveling in the stock cars! This article will explain how to do this for only twenty to thirty dollars.

Memo-Mates

The secret is an integrated-circuit chip developed by Information Storage Devices in San Jose, Calif. No bigger than the head of a thumbtack, it can record up to 20 seconds of sound. This single chip includes a microphone preamplifier, automatic gain control, filter circuits, and a power amplifier.

Although it's possible to obtain these chips from electronics dealers, it's much easier and cheaper to purchase a Memo-Mate. They're sold in Wal-Mart stores, though I got mine from Direct to Retail, 10 California Avenue, Framingham, MA 01701; 800-524-2004. They carried a 10-second version for $19.95 and also two different 20-second versions for $29.95.

The 10-second unit and one of the 20-second versions can record a single message up to the indicated length. The other 20-second version can record as many messages as you can fit in 20 seconds. The single-message versions will repeat the message any time you hit "play." The multiple message unit will play each message in sequence as you hit the play button, but once through the cycle it's necessary to press a reset button for the sequence to begin again.

The single-sound version

I installed a 20-second single-message unit in an Athearn 50-foot double-door boxcar, then recorded the sound of a train in motion, including one whistle sounding. This car is set up to work in two different modes. The circuit is shown in fig. 1.

First, if the slide switch on the bottom of the car is set to LOOP, whatever sound is recorded will be repeated each time the car's wheels make one revolution and the recording has finished playing. In practice this produces continuous sound as long as the car is moving.

If the slide switch is set to the REED position, the recording will play only when a reed switch has been triggered by a trackside magnet. The switch is located to one side of the car for two reasons. I didn't want it to actuate when passing over uncoupling magnets, and I wanted it to be direction-sensitive. If a magnet is set up to trigger a whistle when an eastbound train approaches a crossing, it should not sound the blast when a westbound train passes the same spot.

The multiple-sound version

I installed the multiple-message version in a covered hopper, see fig. 2. It can play a sequence of sounds in order, or it can be arranged to play one sound over and over and then switch to play the rest of the sequence. Each time the PLAY reed switch is actuated, the next sound in the sequence will play. After they have all played, the RESET reed switch is actuated (or a hidden button on top of the car is pressed) and they are ready to play again. Any time the RESET is actuated the device will jump to the beginning of the

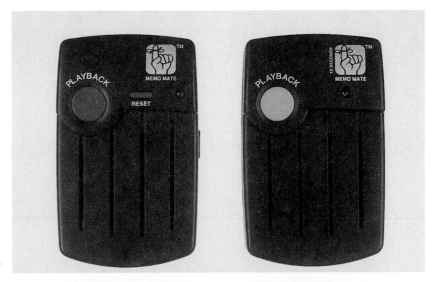

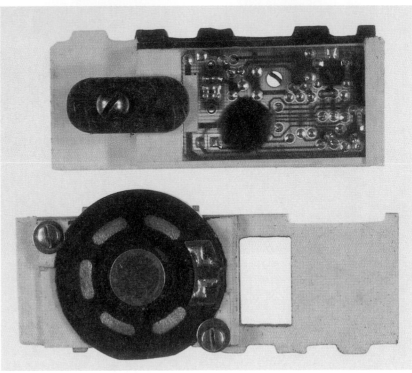

The Memo-Mates are available in 10-second and 20-second versions.

The brass tab on the back of the circuit board enclosure pivots to release the board. The speaker mounts to a similar faceplate behind the opposite door.

FIGURE 1 Single-Sound Version / FIGURE 2 Multiple-Sound Version

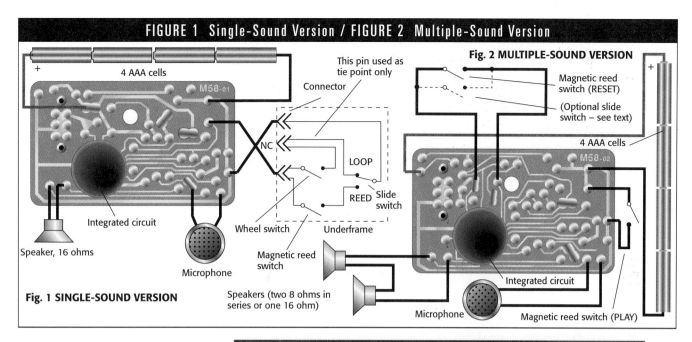

Fig. 2 MULTIPLE-SOUND VERSION

4 AAA cells

M58-01

This pin used as tie point only

Connector

Magnetic reed switch (RESET)

(Optional slide switch – see text)

4 AAA cells

M58-02

NC

LOOP

REED

Slide switch

Wheel switch

Underframe

Magnetic reed switch

Integrated circuit

Fig. 1 SINGLE-SOUND VERSION

Speaker, 16 ohms

Integrated circuit

Microphone

Speakers (two 8 ohms in series or one 16 ohm)

Microphone

Magnetic reed switch (PLAY)

sequence so that the next time PLAY is activated the first sound recorded will be played back.

The optional switch is a miniature slide switch which simply shorts out the reset function so that the unit can be used in the single-message mode. Instead of the switch, you could permanently close the circuit to create a single-message unit, or mount a small magnet within the car to keep the RESET reed switch closed.

I used piezo speakers in this car, one at each end, but they produced too little sound, so I didn't really explore the car's possibilities. However, I think it has potential for a car used in a repetitive turnaround service. For example, you could have the sound of picking up a load of ore, crossing a trestle, dumping the load, crossing the trestle and then reset. Just install a reset magnet before the loading tipple.

Construction

Open up the Memo-Mate and remove the batteries, speaker, microphone, and circuit board. The slide

Here's the overall layout of the boxcar. For long life, Derek used four AAA cells to power his unit. The red object is the microphone.

switch has a small plastic piece that extends to the outside of the case. Save it, because you can probably use it later.

The circuit board is held by a small screw. The microphone and speaker are cemented in place, but a hobby

knife will cut through the adhesive. Clean the adhesive residue from the microphone using acetone or lacquer thinner. Don't unsolder the microphone wires; instead clip them so short leads remain on the microphone and circuit board. This will

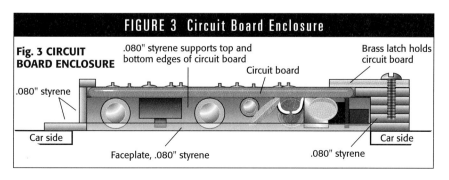

FIGURE 3 Circuit Board Enclosure

Fig. 3 CIRCUIT BOARD ENCLOSURE

.080" styrene supports top and bottom edges of circuit board

Circuit board

Brass latch holds circuit board

.080" styrene

Car side

Faceplate, .080" styrene

.080" styrene

Car side

FIGURE 4 Axle Wipers

Insulating paint covers half the raised pin which completes the circuit once per revolution. The near wiper is in constant contact.

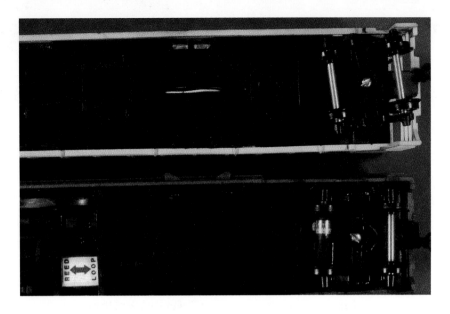

The boxcar's reed switch is visible at the upper edge, to the right of the slide switch. Derek put the hopper's microphone in one of the bays.

help identify the correct circuit points when it's time to wire.

The photos and fig. 3 show my boxcar installation. Simply put, I built a styrene box to hold the circuit board and glued it to a faceplate that fits behind the door opening. Little styrene L-brackets allow this unit to slide into place. Figure 4 shows the electrical wiper I added to one truck.

The speaker was attached to a similar unit. I had to remove part of the floor to clear the bottom edge of my speaker. For the best acoustics, you want the faceplates to fit snugly so the car is almost airtight. I then cut a "port" into the speaker faceplate. Sliding the door across this port allows me to fine-tune the acoustics. I mounted the microphone behind a ¼" hole drilled through the placard holder on the car end.

I hope you'll try building one or more of these sound cars. Set up one to provide continuous locomotive sounds, and another for a whistle, bell, or horn. For a little money, they'll add a great deal of enjoyment. You might even say they're a sound investment.